RHYTHMS

for the

SOUL

A Collection of Poems Inspired by the
Living Word of God
Feeding the Spirit, Mind, and Soul

To Jessica, may God add a blessing to your life from the words of this book!

Mona J Harry

Mona Goodman Harry

ISBN 978-1-0980-4166-3 (paperback)
ISBN 978-1-0980-4167-0 (digital)

Christian Faith Publishing, Inc.
832 Park Avenue
Meadville, PA 16335
www.christianfaithpublishing.com

Printed in the United States of America

I developed a joy for writing when I was in the seventh grade. It all started with *Randy, Peaches and Me*, a story written by my cousin Niece. I can remember many days sitting at the dining room table in my grandparents' house, proofreading every page Niece wrote. There are many who inspired me along the way, but I must say Niece is the beginning of where my writing career is now.

Foreword

As pastor of a growing congregation, being a channel of information, as well as inspiration, is a tall task that can only be accomplished through the help and the hand of God. As you might expect, at times I need inspiration in my own life. Of course, my main source of inspiration are the holy scriptures. However, there are other materials that prove to be valuable sources of personal encouragement as well.

When I read Mona Harry's book *Rhythms for the Soul*, it immediately became another of my favorite resources for motivation and inspiration. It brought joy, laughter, and tears. I have known Mona for well over twenty years, and she has trusted me with personal matters she has experienced and grown from. So when I read the stories and the poems in this book, I knew they were birthed from a real place of personal experience and reflection within her heart and mind.

Truth be told, each of us, at some point in our lives, have or will go through valley experiences that rock us to the core and challenge our faith. Many of the stories from this book are relatable and relevant to anyone who has gone through valleys and come out on the other side of through.

You will really appreciate Mona's transparency throughout this book as it will serve to help others who might encounter the same or similar situations. She has also done a masterful job in relating her stories and poems to biblical characters and passages that gives this book that much more validity and credibility.

I am so honored to write the foreword for this book, and I know it will be a point of reference and reflection now and for many years to come for all who read it.

Vincent H. Riley
Senior Pastor
Meeting Place Church
Charlotte, North Carolina

Preface

We all go through trials and tribulations in life. Some seem so hard we don't know how we will ever make it through. God is a present help, and He will never leave us to fend for ourselves. God has given us His Son, Jesus Christ, His Spirit, and He has given us His true and living word: the Bible.

I have faced many disappointments in life, some hurt to the point it felt as if the very wind was knocked out of me. But God. Everyone has or should have a "But God" experience to share. My "But God" began by writing poetry.

It is often said, if you put rhythm to it, people will learn. We teach our children through rhymes and singing. When I began to listen to God speak, He placed in my heart the desire to teach His Word through poetry. He gave me the title *Rhythms for the Soul.* We must all come to realize that things change. While listening to a message by Dr. Charles Stanley, I was reminded seasons, people, and circumstances change, but there is one thing that will never change: God's Word.

Thinking back to the civil rights movement, We protest, we marched arm in arm, we marched hands up, we laid down, we sat down, we boycotted, we stood up and didn't give up on what we believed in and are still believing in.

We held out for what we knew was and is right, but there is no protesting, no boycotting, no standing up, no sitting down, no laying down, and no holding out in hopes that God's Word will ever change to fit our fleshly desire(s). The Word of God is the beginning and the end, and it will *never* change based on what we feel or think.

Through reading, meditating, and studying God's Word, through tears, fears, anger, sadness, and joy, I can present to you the following pages which will teach of God's love, grace, and mercy. Read, learn, and allow God in your heart.

Acknowledgments

There are so many people I would like to thank for praying for me and with me and for their words of encouragement.

My beautiful mother, Louise G. Goodman, whose sacrifices made me the woman I am today.

My dad, the late Thomas Goodman Jr., who loved me dearly.

My husband, Pomanda, a very talented and gifted man. My children, Amanda who has dreams of becoming a writer also and to my son, William, who is wise beyond his years.

The Goodman, Gibbons, and Harry families and a special thanks to my late mother in-law, Pearl Harry, who was the epitome of forgiveness.

My paternal grandparents: the late Thomas Goodman Sr., a wise and generous man.

The late Thelma B. Goodman, who taught me the meaning of a family praying together.

My maternal grandparents: the late Mattie Gibbons, who was a kind and patient woman, and to William (Jack) Gibbons, a hard-working man. He and my grandma Mattie raised children, grandchildren and one great-grandchild.

My Nellie Bread, my cousin, Shawnell (Nell). Back in the day, this was my ride-or-die chick. We laughed together and we act up together.

Deborah: we adopted each other as sisters; and a special thanks to her family.

The best pastors in my world: Vincent Riley, an example of what it means to be humble, and his wife, Lydia Riley, Pastors David and Melody Burford, who taught me the meaning of faith.

Patricia Hicklin, who, during the time my dad laid in ICU, talked me through one of the toughest days of my life after having an anxiety attack at work.

Patricia Badger, a former manager, who sat with and comforted me at work after receiving the news my dad passed.

Ministers Roxie and Bobby McCorkle who taught me, "If you want God's results, you have to do it God's way."

My cousin, Pastor Raymond Goodman, and his wife, Natalie, for resuscitating me by breathing into me God's Word during sad moments in my life.

I would like to say thanks to my church family. A very special thanks to Minister Bryan and Rosie, Rev. Reginald and his wife, Patricia, and Jasper and Tanja for taking my children under their wings and treating them as their very own.

A special thanks to the ones who woke up my sleeping dreams, S. Kristi Douglass, author of *Portrait of a Princess: The Truth about You from the King's Point of View*; Cassandra O'Neal, author of *Day by Day Faith*; Keesha Gibbons Caldwell, author of *As Only She Knows*; and Mary Ingram McGill, author of *Living in Existence* and Renée Hill Carter, author of *What (staying healthy and whole) About (while you're helping others) Me?* And a special thanks to my Kita, my Madam President, Nikita.

A big thanks to my cousin Tarah, who took time out of her busy life to edit my work. Your talents and expertise are a blessing to me.

Thanks for the Memories

(Inspired by Min. Roxie McCorkle)

My mother was the lone rider. She sometimes traveled up and down a long dark Highway 378. I was a member of my high school marching band, and she would pick me up from school after band practice and football games. No matter what time we return from an away game, she was there waiting for me.

My daddy was always the man that needed forms completed. As a little girl, he would come in my room, and I would pretend to be a secretary sitting at my desk waiting to help him fill out his paperwork.

My granddaddy, Thomas, was always the voice of wisdom, not just for our family but other families as well. "One link of chain can't rattle by itself," he would say. Meaning, sometimes, the best thing to do to avoid arguments is be quiet. He said, "Eventually that other person will be quite once they realize they are talking to themselves." He was also the neighborhood notary republic. Every year around Easter, when *The Ten Commandments* aired, we (his grandchildren) had to be present, sitting on the floor, sitting on the sofa, or sitting on a little wooden chair. It really didn't matter where you sat; you just better be present and account for watching *The Ten Commandments*. And he always had a hot meal waiting for his grandchildren when we arrive home from school.

My grandma, Thelma, was a hardworking woman, and anyone around her had to work hard as well. I remember many Saturday mornings, gathered around the breakfast table praying together, not a simple God is good. God is great type of prayer, but the entire Lord's Prayer before eating together, then cleaning the house from top to bottom together.

A bed didn't dare go unmade and dishes dare not sit in the kitchen sink. We dusted furniture, swept floors, raked pine needles, and raked a dirt driveway. I never understood that, but back in the day, we didn't ask why; we just did it. My older cousins chased and caught chickens in the backyard, wrung the necks, dipped them in a black pot of boiling water so that the feathers could easily be plucked off. I refused to eat chicken at my grandma's house.

My grandma Mattie was a humble woman. She and my grand-daddy William lived in a big board house that stood what seemed to me like ten feet off the ground. There was no indoor plumbing; we use the bathroom in an outhouse and got fresh water from a hand pump. There was no telephone in the house, and one black-and-white TV set sat on a stand in the kitchen. There was no baseboard heat and no AC, and not once did I hear a complaint.

Some days I would go to their house after school, and she as well always had a hot full course meal waiting for her grandchildren. I spent many winter nights there and had to share a bed with my cousins Melissa and Lynn. They would always make me sleep in the middle. I didn't like that because I felt they were looking at me as a baby. But even before, they knew what reversed psychology meant. They would say, "You should be glad. The person in the middle always has cover."

There were walnut and fig trees in their yard. I remember one Christmas getting a red coat with white fur; my granddaddy called me Sana Clause, not Santa Clause.

Despite no indoor plumbing, no telephone, electric heat, nor AC, the happiest times of my life were spent in that big old board house.

My Vision, My Purpose, and My Goal

My vision for *Rhythms for the Soul* is that it's read by people across the world. And for it to be so widely spread and read that it's listed on New York's best sellers list.

My purpose is to show the Word of God is never stale, outdated, nor boring. It's vivid, it's alive, and it's on time. It's real and it's life changing.

My goal is for people to surrender their lives to the One and True Living God, to feel the presence of God in their lives, and to have a personal relationship with God, to prick the hearts of everyone who reads my book to study God's Word.

The Approach

Rhythms for the Soul has been divided into four parts:

"The Backdrop." This section gives the reader a synopsis of the upcoming poem. As with the theater, the backdrop is a part of the stage's scenery.

"The Rhythm." This section is a poem. It's a rhyming scheme, for the most part, that teaches God's Word. And it's a way to prick the heart and encourage readers to study God's Word.

"The Stage Exit." In this section, you will find closing remarks. All performances end with a closing remark.

"Encouragement for the Soul." All writings in this section encourages the soul. This section includes longer passages without rhythm.

A Special Dedication to the Ministers of the Gospel

All I asked...

> Then Jesus went with them to the olive grove called Gethsemane and He said, "sit here while I go over there to pray". He took Peter and Zebedee's two sons; James and John and He became anguished and distressed. He told them, my soul is crushed with grief to the point of death. Stay here and keep watch with me. (Matthew 26:36)

Jesus was placed on this earth to give eternal life to anyone willing to receive. He was a beacon of light in a dark world. He healed the sick and raised the dead. He gave comfort to those grieving and hope to those that were lost. He poured out so much of Himself, but did anyone pour hope, encouragement, or strength back into Him? When Jesus needed His disciples, they fell asleep.

Are we falling asleep on our pastors, reverends, bishops, ministers, and deacons? We go to them for counseling, prayer, and encouragement. But how often are we praying for and encouraging them?

Encouragement for the Soul

Find Significance

I am continuously looking for significance in what I hear during my day-to-day journey because life is a journey. We can make it one where we aimlessly wander around lost, confused, angry, defeated, busted, and discussed. Or, we can choose to look for what is significant in life and make it a learning experience. Be it in what we say and do or be it in what others say or do. Be it in God's Word we read or be it in God's Word He reveals; we should always look for the significant things in life!

Backdrop 1

We sometimes deceive ourselves into believing we are doing exactly what is expected of us to do when it comes to God. We contradict ourselves; we say one thing but do something totally opposite. We have a tendency of saying, "God knows my heart." We say this not because we are being honest or sincere; we say this as a scapegoat to sin.

It is true that God knows our heart. And God knows that we often say this as a means of continuing in our sin. Ask yourself this question: "What shall we say then? Shall we continue in sin that grace may abound?" Certainly not! (Romans 6:1–2). In a nutshell, Paul is saying, God is a merciful God, and He will forgive our sin if we repent, but that's not to say we continue sinning with the mind-set of "All I have to do is ask God to forgive me." And if we continue in sin, Romans 1:28 states, "And even as they did not like to retain God in their knowledge, God gave them over to a debased mind to do those things which are not fitting." God gives us all what is called "a free will," and we make our own choices. His Word is everywhere: churches, TV, radio, and internet ministry. We have no excuse for saying, "I didn't know" or "No one ever told me." With His Word all around us, God expects us to obey; there are no excuses.

Now, put yourself in a comparable situation. How would you feel if someone continued to hurt you? This person knows what they are doing is hurtful; still, they continue to hurt. I've been there, and it doesn't feel good at all.

Tyler Perry wrote a play titled *Madea Goes to Jail*. There was one scene that will forever stay on my mind because his words were true:

"It's not but so many times I can tell you what you do is hurting me before I began to ask, 'do you really love me?'"

My pastor Vincent Riley has a saying: "Your audio ought to match your video." It is my prayer that after reading "From God to Us," you search your heart, and if there be any behavior unpleasing to God, "Make your audio match your video."

Rhythm 1

From God to Us

How can you say you believe in Me, but have no faith in Me?

> Yet in this things ye did not believe the Lord your God. (Deuteronomy 1: 32, KJV)

> Why are you afraid? Do you still have no faith? (Mark 4:40)

How can you say you know Me but have no knowledge of Me?

> My people are destroyed for a lack of knowledge. (Hosea 4:6, NKJV)

How can say you love Me and hate those that were created by Me?

> If someone says, "I Love God," and hates his brother, he is a liar; for he who does not love his brother whom he has seen, how can he love God whom he has not seen? (1 John 4:20, NKJV)

How can you expect things from Me?
Yet you often reject Me.

> Because you have rejected knowledge, I will also
> reject you as my priests; because you have ignored
> the law of your God. (Hosea 4:6, NIV)

> And the Lord told him: "Listen to all that the
> people are saying to you; it is not you they have
> rejected, but me as their king." (1 Samuel 8:7)

How can you say you want Me?
But sometimes won't acknowledge Me.

> My people are doomed because they do not
> acknowledge me. (Hosea 4:6, GNB)

> "But he denied it in front of them all. I don't
> know what you are talking about," he said.
> (Matthew 26:70)

You lift your hands towards Me, only when you need Me.
You bow down before Me, only when you need to receive from
Me.
But truly I believe in you.
I sent My only begotten Son to you.

> For God so love the world that he gave his only
> begotten son, that whoever believes in him shall
> not perish but have everlasting life. (John 3:16)

(Sidebar) I remember growing up as a child attending Asbury
United Methodist Church. Every Sunday the choir would march
down the aisles in their blue robes singing. I could hear Mrs. Catherin
"Cat" English leading "Everlasting Life" and Cousin Lou on the
piano. The entire choir sung with such passion!

"Everlasting life, everlasting life, everlasting life is free.
I'm so glad Jesus gave it to me; everlasting life is free."
Everlasting life was a gift to us but it was the ultimate sacrifice
of Jesus.

And truly I know you
Since it was I that created you.

> And the Lord God formed man of the dust of
> the ground and breathed into his nostrils the
> breath of life; and man became a living being.
> (Genesis 2:7)

> Before I formed you in the womb I knew you.
> Before you were born I sanctified you; I ordained
> you a prophet to the nations. (Jeremiah 1:5)

Never doubt My love for you.
I gave My only begotten Son to the enemy because of you.

> Then He came the third time and said to them
> "The hour has come; behold, the Son of Man is
> being betrayed into the hands of sinners. Rise let
> us be going. See, My betrayer is at hand." (Mark
> 14:41–44)

Know that you may always come to Me.
My plan is to prosper thee.

> Beloved, I pray that in every way you may suc-
> ceed in all things and be in good health, just as
> your soul prospers. (3 John 1:2, NIV)

> For I know the thoughts that I think toward you,
> says the Lord, thoughts of peace and not of evil,
> to give you a future and a hope. (Jeremiah 29:11)

Feel secure in Me wanting you.
My heavens were created so I may be with you.

> Let not your heart be troubled; you believe in
> God, believe also in Me. In My Father's house are
> many mansions; if it were not so, I would have
> told you. I go to prepare a place for you. And
> if I go and prepare a place for you, I will come
> again and receive you to Myself; that where I go
> you know, and the way you know. (John 14:1–4,
> NKJV)

Lift your hands to praise Me
Not just in need from Me
Bow down to worship Me and know
I have already saved thee.

Stage Exit

We all have sinned and fallen short of the glory of God. Take the time to say, "God, if there be anything in me that is not like You, I ask that You reveal it to me. Then I ask that You give me the strength to remove everything that is not like You and that doesn't bring You the glory; it is in the name of Jesus Christ I pray. Amen."

Backdrop 2

Many years ago, I was in church during watch night service. The minister began speaking of how time after time, we push God aside and fail to take time out of our busy schedule to commune with Him. I don't remember exactly what was said, but I remember asking God to forgive me for not spending time with Him and for not giving Him praise. I praised Him for giving me chance after chance despite who I was. There is a song by Rev. Luther Barnes I enjoy listening too; it's titled "God of another Chance." I can very well relate to that because as Rev. Barnes says in the song, we blew our second chance so, so long ago.

Rhythm 2

It Was Brought to My Attention

It was brought to my attention I must apologize to You
For all the times I did other things except spend time with You.
You waited in my home and met me on my job
I rushed by You so quickly, no time to realize
That unforeseen dangers I face each and every day,
You gave your angels charge to guide me on my way.
It was brought to my attention I often neglect You
Your Word sits on my shelf untouched; I have so much to do.
That little voice I hear, that whispers oh so clear
Beckons me draw near, cast all my cares and fears.
When it was brought to my attention Your presence had filled the room
My body, spirit, soul, and mind repented for all those times.
In shock of my behavior, I bowed to my Lord and Savior
The tears filled my eyes, my heart was sick inside.
How could I be so blind, to ignore You time after time
Despite dishonor in me, you keep seeing favor in me
And gave me another chance to repent from my sin.
Now, you have my attention; I acknowledge You in all my ways
From hence forth and forevermore, from You I will not stray.

Stage Exit

God is always with us. The problem is we aren't always with Him.

> Therefore go and make disciples of all nations, baptizing them in the name of the Father, the Son and the Holy Spirit, and teaching them to obey. And surely, I am with you always, to the very end of the age. (Matthew 28:19–20)

Now, take notice of these conditions:

1. Make disciples of all nations and baptize. Back in the day, a popular television show called *Mission Impossible* began with a recorded message to an agent: "Your mission _____, should you choose to accept it."

    Put your name in the blank space and know that God has a mission for all that is called by His name, if we choose to accept it. The message ended by saying: This message will self-destruct in five seconds. Accepting the mission is a choice. God will not force us. But realize this: choosing not to accept God will self-destruct our lives. Why? Because it was self that chose not to accept the mission. Therefore, to go make disciples and baptize, we must do this: accept Jesus Christ as our Lord and Savior.

2. Teach obedience (to teach obedience, we must first be obedient).
3. This all comes with spending time with God.

    > So do not fear, *for I am with you*; do not be dismayed, for I am your God. (Isaiah 41:10, NKJV)

If I go up to the heavens, *you are there*; if I make my bed in the depths, *you are there*. (Psalm 139:8, NIV)

Yet I have this against you. You have forsaken the love you had at first. (Revelations 2:4)

Stop and reflect on the time you accepted Jesus Christ as your Lord and Savior. Wasn't it a wonderful feeling? As with me, you probably read your Bible all the time, including committing to a "Read Your Bible in a Year" chart. You were at the church every time the doors opened. These are the very moments we need to get back to. We exit the stage proclaiming to bring God back to our attention.

By and By

(Inspired by Bishop T.D. Jakes)

There is an old Gospel song titled "We'll Understand it Better By and By." After listening to a sermon by Bishop T.D. Jakes, I now understand that song much better. God is the Alpha and the Omega, the beginning and the end (Revelations 21:6). God knew us before we were formed in the womb (Jeremiah 1:5). God was here before the foundation of the world (Genesis 1). With that being said, God knew what would happen to us before it happened. That's not to say everything that happened to us was God's plan for our life.

> For I know the thoughts that I think toward you,
> says the Lord, thoughts of peace and not of evil,
> to give you a future and a hope. (Jeremiah 29:11,
> NKJV)

The earth has existed for thousands upon thousands of years. We face loss of family members, either through a tragic loss, natural cause, or through an illness. God knew from the beginning of time this would happen. After such loss, we find ourselves asking, "Why?" We wonder, "Why didn't God stop this?"

What I learned was this: we are trying to understand in one day, one month, or maybe even years what was in the makings for thousands upon thousands of years. We have shed many tears, and we may not understand it now. God said He will wipe every tear from our eyes (Revelation 21:4); and we will understand it better as time goes by (John 13:7; 1 Corinthians 13:12). It may be on this side of heaven or it may be on the other side, but we will understand it better by and by. This may or may not bring comfort to those who faced or is facing loss or hard times. What happened was known since the beginning of time. We must remember that, although God knew what would happen (loss or pain) it was not his will. This is the thing; we are trying to understand in moments what was in the making thousands of years ago.

Backdrop 3

Proverbs 18:21 says, "Death and life are in the power of the tongue." The tongue is a small member of the body, but it is powerful. What we say to others can either cut them to pieces or it can bandage their wounds.

The fastest mode of transportation known to mankind is not an airplane, a Learjet, a car or speed boat, but the words brought from our mouths. Words travel in a distance that could do us harm or they could do us good. Our words weigh heavily on lives and our well-being; therefore, we must be careful of the words we speak in our own lives and the lives of others.

Watch your thoughts, they become words;
Watch your words, they become actions;
Watch your actions, they become habits;
Watch your habits, they become character;
Watch your character, for it becomes your destiny.

—Frank Outlaw
Late president of the BI-LO stores

Rhythm 3

I Will

I will speak life into my situation and cease my situation from speaking death into me

The enemy has set forth to devour my home and destroy all that God has planned for me

I will speak love into my circumstances and not let my circumstances speak hate into me

That old dragon has breathed forth his fire in attempts to consume me

I will speak faith into my misfortunes and not let my misfortunes speak doubt into me

Satan is continuously busy trying to take away that which the eye cannot see

I will shout victory throughout my home and not let defeat sound from room to room

I will walk by faith and not by sight

The Lord God is forever on the throne

Stage Exit

> Now David was greatly distressed, for the people
> spoke of stoning him. (1 Samuel 30:6, NIV)

But David strengthened *himself* in the Lord, his God. David was a mighty king and a giant killer. But that same David, who, at returning from battle, the people chanted, "Saul has slain his thousands, and David his tens of thousands," this same David is now distressed.

People at times will try to bring you down. Things in life will not always go according to plan. And there will be times when that call for help goes unanswered. In these cases, we must learn to speak life to our spirit.

Backdrop 4

The first chapter of John 1:1 tells us, "In the beginning was the Word and the word was with God and the word was God." Jesus Christ is God in the flesh, which means Jesus is the word in the flesh. When Jesus was tempted by Satan (Matthew 4:1–11) with everything the enemy came at him with, He replied, "It is written."

The Word of God is our weapon against the enemy's tricks. "If thou be the Son of God, command that these stones be made bread, Jesus replied, it is written Man shall not live by bread alone but by every word that proceeded out of the mouth of God. If thou be the Son of God cast thyself down: for it is written, He shall give his angels charge concerning thee." (Matthew 4:6) This was a significant statement made by Satan. Why, you ask? Because it proves that even Satan knows the Word of God, and not only knows the Word but recognizes the Word in the flesh.

> Jesus replied, "It is written again, thou shalt not tempt the Lord thy God." After taking Jesus to a high mountain and showing Jesus all the Kingdoms, Satan said, "All these things will I give thee, if thou wilt fall down and worship me." Again, Jesus replied, it is written, thou shalt worship the Lord thy God and Him only shalt thou serve." (Matthew 4:10)

Another significant piece of information here; you must know who you are in Jesus Christ. How foolish of Satan to offer Jesus that which he already had; all the kingdoms of God.

Second Timothy 2:15 states we must study the Word of God to show ourselves approved. Jesus, being the living Word of God, has been approved, and so are we who are in Christ Jesus. Before we can believe, we must have knowledge or be familiar with what we are believing in.

To know something about someone, we must spend time with them. If you believe in nothing else, believe in the living Word of God.

Rhythm 4

I Believe

I believe in Your word created to flesh
Born in this world to redeem us from death
I believe in Your word manifested through Christ
Deliverance to the way, the truth and the life
I believe Your word walked free of sin, removing the curse
So, blessings will reign
I believe in Your word and the touch of Your hand
To heal and set free the bondage of man
I believe in the stripes Your body bore for me,
Each strike You endured was coverage for me
I believe in the purchase You made for me
The shedding of Your blood cleansed all diseases
I believe in the cross You hung from and died
And rejoiced in the day Your body rised
I believe in salvation that brings liberty
I believe in the strips Your body bore for me.

Stage Exit

Believing brings forth hope, for if we have nothing we believe in, we have nothing to hope for. The Word of God says we have a hope and a future.

The future is what we can't see. But we can believe that a bright and prosperous future is in store for us; the Word of God tells us so. The saints of old said, "I don't know what the future holds but I do *know* (placing emphasis on the word know because it's personal; as in, I spend time with God, we have an intimate relationship; therefore, I know him) who holds the future."

I was inspired to write this poem during a family member, as well as close friend, battle with breast cancer, Angela Gee. She lost the battle but won the war because she is now resting in the bosom of Jesus Christ.

Small Beginnings

Do not despise these small beginnings, for the
Lord rejoices to see the work begin.

—Zechariah 4:10 (NLT)

We are told to dream big but are not told to begin small. When we hear dream big, our mind-set tells us begin big. That's not the case. We start from the ground and then build up. Anything, in my opinion, that starts at the top will soon crash because there is no solid foundation or roots tobuild on.

My dream and my heart's desire was to publish a book of poetry teaching the Word of God. If you are reading this, it means my dream has come to past! I have been writing since 1999. There were times when I wrote three poems and more per week. Then there were times when I went one year or longer and wrote absolutely nothing.

I now have a new perspective for reaching a goal: "With each stroke of the brush you begin to see the big picture." It all starts at the beginning, and it all starts small. You must be willing to start at the bottom or the beginning.

I have yet to see the roof built first on a house.

I have yet to see branches grow first on a tree.

I have yet to see an adult before he/she was a baby.

Always dream big but realize you must start small. Never give up on your dream(s), and by all means, please have one. Dreams bring hope and passion to life.

Backdrop 5

There were times when I read God's Word and was really confused. For instance, Genesis 1:26 says, "So God created man in His own image in the image of God He created him male and female He created them." Jeremiah 1:5 says, "Before I formed you in the womb, I knew you, before you were born, I set you apart; I appointed you as a prophet to the nations." This confused me because I couldn't understand how God created them male and female and Adam and Eve hadn't been created yet and how He knew Jeremiah before he was born.

I prayed and asked God to help me understand, and He did (sidebar: when you don't understand God's Word, ask for guidance and understanding, and He will minister to you). God explained that human life begins as a spirit (a female spirit and a male spirit). That spirit is then placed in a body; so we start out as being a spirit with God. This is how He knew us before we were formed in the womb. He created the spirit before He created flesh. This is also how He knew Jeremiah before he was even formed in his mother's womb.

Continuing in Genesis 1:28, God spoke to the spirit of mankind, male and female. "Then God blessed them, and God said to them, be fruitful and multiply; fill the earth and subdue it; have dominion over the fish of the sea, over the birds of the air and over every living thing that moves on the earth." So even before mankind became flesh, God spoke to the spirit. After gaining this revelation knowledge, God gave me the poem, "You Always Were."

Rhythm 5

You Always Were

You always were since the beginning of time
An important part of God's awesome mind
Before you were formed in your mother's womb
You were of spirit with God in a holy cocoon
As life goes on at an appointed time
God placed your spirit in a vessel of time
God knows the plan He has for your life
Peace and prosperity, joy and not strife
No plans of evil, no plans of defeat
Plans for a future that far exceeds
Any thoughts you may think, any ways you may perceive
Will never compare to God supplying your need
His thoughts are not your thoughts
His ways are not your ways
They are higher than the heavens;
Greater than you can imagine
You always were since the beginning of time
An important part of God's awesome mind
A chosen generation; royal priesthood for all nations

A free will God gives for man to adhere
To the spirit inside to lead and to guide
To the spirit in man to reject worldly plans

Stage Exit

The spirit of mankind shall live for an eternity. God spoke to our spirit before we became flesh. As we exit this stage, remember, invest in that which will live forever: our spirit. What do I mean when I say invest? It means to feed your spirit man. We feed our physical bodies every day, but the spirit is quite often starving, becoming weak.

Backdrop 6

God spoke to Moses one day and told him to go to Pharaoh and tell him, "Let my people go." Exodus chapter 3 gives an account of God's instructions to Moses with assisting in leading the Israelites out of bondage. Moses's question to God was "Who should I say sent me?" God replied, "I Am that I Am" (Exodus 3:14).

God is whatever and whoever we need Him to be. He will be a spouse to the widow and widower, a mother to the motherless and father to the fatherless, a sister or brother or a friend who will never leave us nor forsake you. He is our way out of no way; He is our everything.

Rhythm 6

I Am

You are many things to many people
You are the great I Am!
You never sleep nor slumber
You are the great I Am!
You make a way when we see no way
You are the great I Am!
You are all seeing and all knowing
You are the great I Am!
You have never left me nor forsook me
You are the great I Am!
You lead me, and you guide me
You are the great I Am!
You command grace and mercy to follow me
You are the great I Am!
You sent Jesus to redeem your people
You are the great I Am!

Stage Exit

I Am is followed by a _____. God is what we need Him to be. Don't read what isn't being said. God isn't our selfish ways.

He is Omnipotent (He can do anything but fail), omnipresent (He is everywhere at once), and omniscient (He is all knowing). Who wouldn't serve a God like this?

Use It or Lose It

Inspired by Jentezen Franklin

I heard a motivational sermon one day titled "Accept what is, let go of what was." A portion of the sermon tells an interesting fact about birds in New Zealand and how 43 percent of the birds have wings but can't fly. The reason why is because there are no predators to chase after these birds; therefore they find safety on the ground and never use their God-given gift. The entire sermon (consisting of various speakers) is inspirational. I have included the website. Check it out; it makes for good listening.

God is no respecter of person; therefore, He has instilled in each of us gifts and talents. Some of us realize our gifts and/or talents. But some of us are still searching. First Peter 4:10, NIV says, "Each of you should use *whatever* gift you have received to serve others, as faithful stewards of God's grace in its various forms." And just to be clear, your gift isn't necessarily singing or dancing. Your gift could be detailing cars or cooking or working with children, making arts and crafts. Your gift may be patience. Whatever your gift is, the Word of God tells us to use it for His glory.

Now if you have a gift or talent and you choose to hide it and not let your light shine, it will be taken from you as with the parable Jesus told in Matthew 25:14–30. It should be a familiar passage of scripture, but if not, please read what happens when gifts and talents aren't used. Some may say, "I don't know what I am gifted to do." Well, seek God first and He will show you. Sometimes it's whatever a person is passionate about. I am passionate about writing, so, I knew my gift was in writing. At any rate, do not be like the birds of New Zealand; you have wings but fail to realize you can fly. Don't allow your gifts and talents to lay dormant. (https://www.youtube.com/watch?v=3k56OXvbcjQ)

Backdrop 7

While ministering one Sunday morning, Pastor Vincent Riley made this statement: "The only way to God is through."

Life is filled with challenges. We often try many ways to overcome them or bypass them. Everything we face, Almighty God is the answer. There is only one way to get to the answer. Just because this is a new day and time, don't be deceived into thinking God can't handle it. There is an old cliché that stands true: "There is nothing new under the sun." Whatever it is we face, the Bible has the answer.

Rhythm 7

The Only Way Is Through

His mountains are so high; you can't get over them
His valleys are so low; you can't get under them
His borders are so wide; you can't get around them
The only way to Him is through
Mountains may shake; Jesus make no mistakes
Valleys may flood; Jesus is filled with love
As far as the east sets from the west
Only through Jesus; He removes all transgression
Jesus is the way, the truth, and the life
Only through Him will we have eternal life

Stage Exit

I have heard it said, "There are many ways to God." Well, if you don't serve a Genesis 1:1, John 1:1–5, John 3:16, or Revelation 22:13 (just to name a few) God, I am here to burst your sinking bubble. It ain't but one way; yes, I said ain't. Paul said, "I do not want you to be ignorant of this mystery, brothers and sisters, so that you may not be conceited" (Romans 11:25–26, NIV). In a nutshell, some preach a Gospel different than the true Gospel of Jesus Christ and then boast in a false god. The only way is through believing in Jesus Christ, born of a virgin, walked this earth sinless, was crucified, died, buried, rose from the dead, and is now seated at the right hand of God the Father.

Backdrop 8

God is never changing, and anyone who encounters Him has no other choice but to change. In Matthew 8:20, Jesus said, "Foxes have holes and birds have nest, but the Son of Man has no place to lay his head." I wondered why Jesus had no place to lie down other than outside with the ground for His bed and a possible rock for His pillow. What happened to the multitude of people that followed Him? What happened to the five thousand he fed with two fish and five loaves of bread? Why didn't one of them give Jesus and the disciples a place to sleep?

As I wonder why, God provided the answer through TV ministry. The answer is found in the first sentence of the above paragraph. Once you encounter Jesus, you have no choice but to change. So often, we are so consumed with our lives and what feels good to us or what makes us happy that we don't want to change. We feel as though we are missing out on something fun and exciting if we allow Jesus in our lives and our heart. That couldn't be more wrong. Some of us don't want change; we want what we want when we want it. The mind-set is "Give me just a little bit to get by, help me out of this situation, God, and I won't bother you again" until another crisis arise. Once you encounter Jesus, your life must change. All the things you see as fun that doesn't glorify God must stop. Many people didn't invite Jesus and the disciples into their homes to stay. Why? Because they didn't want Jesus to "clean house." The presence or even the mention of Jesus's name should bring about conviction. If it doesn't (I like the way my friend Brother Larry put it), "it's time to look at yourself in your spiritual mirror."

The following poem was inspired by Matthew 8:20.

Rhythm 8

Holes and Nest

If foxes have holes; And birds have nest
Why has the Son of Man nowhere to rest?
From the rising of the sun; To the going down of the same
The name of the Lord is worthy to be praised
He gives sight to the blind and movement to the lame
He fed multitudes of people; Heals all manner of diseases
If foxes have holes and birds have nest
Why has the Son of Man nowhere to rest?
He cast out demons; He restores the feeble
He mends a broken heart; He gives hope to the lost
If foxes have holes and birds have nest
Why has the Son of Man nowhere to rest?
If the truth be told, we can be as solid as stones
Set in our ways, unbroken, unchanged
Foxes have holes, and birds have nest
Will you give the Son of Man a place to rest?
Rest in your spirit; Rest in your soul
Behold; He stands knocking at the door
Allow Him to come in, changing wrong to right
Give Him a place to rest in your life.

Stage Exit

Before we exit the stage, make a choice today. Open the door and let Jesus come in.

> Listen! I stand at the door and knock; if anyone
> hears my voice and opens the door, I will come
> in and eat with them and they will eat with me.
> (Revelations 3:20)

Allow Jesus into your house so that He can clean it from top to bottom, inside and out. Your life will change forever and for the better.

Be Careful What You Speak

"What is your request?" he asked. She replied, "In your
Kingdom, please let my two sons sit in places of honor next to
you, one on your right and the other on your left." But Jesus
answered by saying to them, "You don't know what you are
asking! Are you able to drink from the bitter cup of suffering
I am about to drink?" "Oh yes, they replied, we are able!"

—Matthew 20:21–22

We ask God for things, but are we truly ready for what we are ask-
ing for? A lot of times we see the end results but didn't take into
consideration the path it took to get to the end. Everything is not
done instantly, and for the most part, my generation and prior real-
ize this. Many people want a position of leading others but refuse
to be led. Remember: small beginnings. Sometimes it's necessary to
go the extra mile. Matthew 5:41 says if a soldier demand that you
carry his gear for a mile, carry it two miles. Well, we may have a bit
of a problem here because some aren't willing to carry the gear for
any distance. The attitude here is often, "Who do you think you are
telling me what to do?" So before we ask, first count the cost of what
it takes to accomplish it. It may mean working longer hours, it may
mean giving up pleasures, and most definitely, it means obedience.

Another thought that comes to mind is being careful with our
words, being careful what we say. Did you know that Jesus had to be
so careful with what He said, even His thoughts? Whatever He said
and even thought came to pass. Mark 11:12 tells Jesus was hungry

and saw a fig tree, but there were no figs on the tree. He spoke to the fig tree saying, "May no one ever eat your fruit again!" The next day when Jesus and the disciples came to the fig tree, it had withered. He spoke it and it was. What we speak, negative or positive, may not manifest itself immediately, but in time, there is the possibility it will.

Backdrop 9

Quite often we hear, "I need a miracle." And it's true. So many of us need so many things. Sometimes it's a miracle of healing or finances. Sometimes it's freedom from addictions or a loved one being saved. Sometimes it's freedom from unforgiveness, anger, or bitterness. Whatever it is, we have a need. But sometimes, God needs us to be a miracle for someone, and by being a miracle, we open a door to receive a miracle. We think a miracle must be something big and out of this world. Not so. Miracles are the unnoticed things we do daily. Keep reading.

Rhythm 9

I Need

I need your eyes, so I can see the weary and the burden to set them free

I need your arms to extend to the lost and pull them back to the sign of the cross

I need your hands, so I can feel the hurt and the broken that they may be healed

I need your mouth, so I can speak words of encouragement to hopelessness and defeat

I need your feet to search and find the faint and the weak for thy too are mine

I need your heart to show true love at no cost, to show the meaning of my death on the cross

I need your love, so the world can feel my burial and resurrection most certainly, is real.

Stage Exit

And there you have it. A miracle is not only parting a sea, loaves and fishes, walking on water, or raising the dead. A miracle is what we do on a day-to-day basis. A simple smile can be someone's miracle.

Backdrop 10

In the book of 1 Samuel 13:14, the Bible tells of King David being a man after the heart of God. But how could this be? Wasn't David the one who committed adultery? Wasn't David the one who had his mistress's husband killed? It's all written in 2 Samuel chapters 11–12.

The Bible tells of how King David schemed and plotted to cover up his affair with Bathsheba all while her husband, Uriah, was on the battlefield fighting. While his men were in battle, David was home. He stood on his rooftop, saw a beautiful woman, and desired her. He sent for her, slept with her, and she became pregnant. To cover up their sin, David called Uriah off the battlefield and commanded he return home. David's plan was for Uriah to accept the offer to return home and sleep with his wife whom he, chances are, haven't seen in a while. So we can read between the lines of scripture and know where David's plot was headed.

But Uriah was a man of honor and refused to go home and relax while other men were still on the battlefield. Seeing that Uriah refused to go home, David knew he had to come up with another plan. He sent word to the battlefield to have Uriah placed on the frontline in hopes he would be killed in battle; David's plan worked. How could a man after God's own heart have a heart to do such a thing?

Many of the psalm were written by David. Time after time we read how David cries out to God for grace and mercy. Time spent with praising and acknowledging God was what made David "a man after God's own heart." We all have sinned and fallen short of God's callings. The important thing is to cry out to God asking for forgiveness, grace, and mercy and deciding to walk away from that sin. God is a just God and will hear our cries. Another thing to remember is that God doesn't deliver us so that we can continue in sin. Romans 6:1–2 says, "What shall we say then? Shall we continue in sin, that grace may abound? God forbids. How shall we that are dead to sin, live any longer therein?"

Rhythm 10

A Sinner's Way Out

The world is laden with sin
And we often give in
To the things of the flesh
And to what we think is best
We seldom stop to realize
That if we remain in sin, we will die
Giving into the flesh
Sometimes mean our last breath
The Bible records this and it's true
King David was of God but sinned too
He spied on a beautiful matron
He desired to make her his lady
Although she belonged to another
He desired to make her his lover
King David must now debate
How to get rid of her mate
He must find a way out, a cover-up
That's what sin is about
He plotted to have the man killed
Then this lady could legally be his
And the world would never know
Of his undercover show
But somehow during his plan

David's mind did not comprehend
There was One who knew his thoughts
Aware of his secret plot
His wife gave birth to a son
That was sick, and David found none
That could relive the child of his pain
So, David prayed to no end
He fast day and night
That God would give the child life
But David's decision displeased the Lord
And it cost him his baby boy
Be careful of your way out
Of the sin that has you encamped about
Tell God your secret thoughts
He will cleanse you of unrighteous thoughts
While on bended knees, confess to God
All your wrong deeds
Repent with all your heart
Sinner, that's the only way out.

Stage Exit

As we exit the stage, we see that King David, a mighty man of God, schemed, plotted, and set up an innocent man to be killed all for his personal desires and lust. This type of behavior is present in the world today. Always remember and don't ever forget: things done in the dark will eventually find its way to the light. It's called exposure.

> For all that is secret will eventually be brought into the open, and everything that is concealed will be brought to light and made known to all. (Luke 8:17)

It's Not Everything

Food in the stomach and shelter over the head isn't everything. Now don't get me wrong and hear what I am not saying. These things are vital for life, but it isn't everything needed in life. Allow me to go a bit deeper to give a better understanding of where I am coming from.

While in Egypt, the Israelites had food to eat, clothes to wear, and a shelter over their heads. Matthew 4:4 supports my statement. "No! People do not live by bread alone, but by every word that comes from the mouth of God." The Israelites cried out to God because of how they were treated. They didn't say, "Oh God, help us. We are hungry. Oh God, help us. We have no place to lay our heads." Nor did they say, "Oh God, help us, we are naked." But what the Bible indicated they did say was, "Oh God, help us. Our slave masters are harsh."

What we must remember from reading the Bible is the Egyptians were harsh people. Pharaoh commanded male babies be killed from the moment they came out of the womb. When that didn't work, he commanded once they were born, they be thrown into the river.

Therefore, what the Israelites needed was far more than what they were getting. They needed to be delivered from a life of oppression and depression. They needed peace and comfort. Peace of mind cannot be brought and can only truly come from having a relationship with God the Father. Don't allow yourself to believe that because "I provide a roof over their heads, clothes on their backs and food in their stomach," that's all they need. Or "Only these things are important."

I beg to differ. What we need above all these things is a relationship with God. Had it not been for the relationship the Israelites forefathers Abraham, Isaac, and Jacob had with God, He would not have heard their cries. Exodus 3:6–7 says, "I am the God of your father, the God of Abraham, the God of Isaac, and the God of Jacob. I have certainly seen the oppression of my people in Egypt. I have heard their cries of distress because of their harsh slave drivers." Notice, God said, "my people."

My takeaway from this is although they (the Israelites) received what the flesh needed, they were starving for what the spirit needed. My friend, recognize this: it's not all about providing what the flesh needs. I posed the question "Are you providing the peace a mind needs and are you providing what the soul needs?" In no way am I saying we are God. What I am saying is this: don't make life hard for people. Don't be what causes oppression and/or depression nor what causes stress. Don't use as a scapegoat "Well, if they have God in their life, then what I do won't bother them."

Let's go to the scriptures. There were many people in the Bible that had God in their lives but became overwhelmed. I will list a few: Moses, King David, Elijah, Gideon, Daniel, the disciples, and Paul, just to name a few. In a nutshell, don't be a stumbling block in anyone's life. Instead, help with being a stepping-stone or a bridge over troubled waters.

Backdrop 11

Your word is a lamp for my feet, a light on my path.

—Psalm 119:105

A lighthouse is a tower, building, or other type of structure designed to emit light from a system of lamps and lenses and to serve as a navigational aid. I used a lighthouse as a metaphor for being in a dark place in life and taking the Word of God as a light to bring us out of darkness.

Rhythm 11

Lighthouse
(Inspired by Pastor Melody Burford)

When I make it to the Lighthouse
I know everything will be alright
As it stands right now
I'm surrounded by the night
The cargo I carry is heavy
And sometimes cause me to tarry
In a place I wish not to be
But as it stands right now
Darkness is all I can see
As I drift along through the night
Darkness is pierce with Light
Standing tall across the way
The Lighthouse shines like day
So, in my mind I imagine
This lighthouse that I see
As being the true and living word of God
Which will always guide and comfort me.

Stage Exit

The lighthouse is symbolic to Christians being a light in a dark world. If all of us let our little light shine, we will bring forth a marvelous light to this world. There are more with us, (the people of God), than with Satan. It's time we took authority of the power we have in numbers and rule out the darkness in this world.

I would like to share with you a teaching by the late Bishop Phillip Davis. Bishop Davis explained, when Revelations 12:3–4, 7–9 took place, Lucifer (Satan) rebelled against God and because of his rebellion, was kicked out of heaven. Bishop Davis taught that we are the majority. Now, there is no scripture that specifically states this; we read in Revelation 12 one-third of the stars were thrown to the earth. We also read in 2 Kings 6:16: "Those who are with us are more than those against us."

> Then I witnessed in heaven another significant event. I saw a large red dragon with seven heads and ten horns, with seven crowns on his heads. His tail swept away one-third of the stars in the sky and he threw them to the earth. (Revelation 12:3–4)

> Then there was war in heaven. Michael and his angels fought against the dragon and his angels. And the dragon lost the battle, and he and his angles were forced out of heaven. (Revelation 7–9)

> Jesus replied, "I saw Satan fall like lightening from heaven." (Luke 10:18)

The above scriptures support my belief that we, God's people, are the majority.

Backdrop 12

But mark this: There will be terrible times in the last days. People will be lovers of themselves, lovers of money, boastful, proud, abusive, and disobedient to their parents, ungrateful, unholy, Without love, unforgiving, slanderous, without self-control, brutal, not lovers of the good, Treacherous, rash, conceited, lovers of pleasure rather than lovers of God—having a form of godliness but denying its power. Have nothing to do with such people. (2 Timothy 3:1–5, NIV)

Be sober, be vigilant; because your adversary, the devil, walks about like a roaring lion, seeking whom he may devour. (1 Peter 5:8)

While listening to Bishop T.D. Jakes, he asked the question, "Where are your children?" Driving at the point, we make it our business to know where our children are physically, but how much effort do we make knowing where they are mentally? With so much going on in the world today, communication is vital for survival. We can't assume that just because our kids are home and in their rooms, everything is okay. Isolation can be a silent killer, and it is important to remain on guard and have discerning spirits.

It was reported that the Columbine shooters spent a lot of time in their rooms playing gun-related video games. And although there is no ironclad proof that this is what led to the shootings, the concern is the amount of time spent playing violent games. Be vigilant and take notice when things just don't seem right.

Rhythm 12

How Much
(Inspired by the Columbine
High School Shooting)

How much longer will we stand by watching the lambs of God
Continue to die? Not because He has called them home but
Because Satan roams. How many more lives must we lose?
Before the saints of God make their move. To march into the
Enemy's camp and demand that he gives us our children back.
How much longer will we stand by and let Satan's Kingdom
Continue to rise? God has given us what we need to bring the
Devil to his knees. To place his existence under our feet and
Cease his constant and continual defeat.
When will it stop?
When will it end?
Or will we sit by and let Satan win?
When will we rise as Jesus rose and proclaim God's Word
Before the foe?

Stage Exit

We exit this stage with heavy hearts because there has been
over a decade and a half of senseless school and other shootings. Our

nation fails to realize this truth; when God is removed, it gives the enemy open range in this world.

Bring God back, and it will bring an end to the constant attacks. Remember: God's people are the majority with the authority.

Even the Demons

Psalm 91:11–13 proclaims, "For he will order his angels to protect you wherever you go. They will hold you up with their hands, you won't even hurt your foot on a stone."

> Then the devil took him to Jerusalem to the highest point of the temple and said, if you are the son of God jump off! For the scriptures say he will order his angels to protect and guard you. And they will hold you up with their hands, so you won't even hurt your foot on a stone. (Luke 4:9–11)

Even demons know the Word of God. Do you?

> When Jesus arrived on the other side of the lake, in the region of the Gadarenes, two men who were possessed by demons met him. They came out of the tombs and were so violent that no one could go through that area. They began screaming at him, why are you interfering with us, Son of God? (Matthew 8:28–29)

Even the demons recognize the Son of God. Do you?

The scripture goes on to say, "Have you come to torture us before God's appointed time?"

Even the demons know the plans God has for them. Do you know the plans God has for you?

> You believe that there is one God; Good! Even the demons believe that, and shudder. (James 2:19)

So if you believe that there is One God and the demons believe that there is One God, what makes what you believe different than what the demons believe, hmm?

> One day the members of the heavenly court came to present themselves before the Lord and Satan came also with among them. (Job 1:6)

Even the demons present themselves before God. Do you?

Backdrop 13

There was, at one point in my life, a time of uncertainty. It was a time of not knowing who I was. I didn't have the relationship with God back then that I have now. I didn't know who to turn to or what to believe. I heard the spiritual enemy saying things that put doubt in my mind and left me questioning everything I thought was true. One person was spreading rumors, and even one close to me fed into the rumors. These rumors kept me in a secret dark place for a long time. My relief: a pen and paper to write what I was feeling but didn't have the courage to say. When you go through dark times in life, be still and attentive because God has a way of bringing you out of the darkness.

Jekalyn Carr said, "Whatever the devil say I am, I declare I'm not and whatever the devil says I'm not, I declare I am."

Rhythm 13

Secret Place

In my secret place there is much heartache and pain
And to the ones I love the most I cannot even begin to explain
It's like a yoke around my neck and a burden on my back
I pray to God in heaven for peace to keep my soul in tack.
In my secret place you will find many tears
If I could keep them in one place you will see a river flow from here
I pray to God for comfort and relief from all my fears
If I had wings like an eagle, I would fly away from here
But that could never happen because my secret place lies within me
It has made a home in my heart and from it I cannot part
In my secret place I store thoughts I wish to say
But I have so little courage in my heart is where they stay
I know God is a comforter and He knows our deepest thought
That secret place I hold inside must soon reveal itself
I cast my cares and fears on Him for his love will never part.

Stage Exit

Although she's no longer with us, I will forever be grateful to my grandma Thelma who gave me the earthy strength to face my uncertainty. At about the age of twenty-eight, I went to her house crying like a baby. Her words to me that day were "Pull yourself together."

Her stern yet loving words gave me the courage I needed to face my fears.

I will also be forever grateful to a longtime friend, Lillian Whack. Lillian gave her testimony one day during a Children's Ministry Meeting. Her testimony many, many years ago set me free!

With that being said, I found freedom! Don't stop reading now. There's more to come.

Backdrop 14

Franklin D. Roosevelt stated, "The only thing we have to fear is fear itself."

My road to freedom was a long dark road. But I am free, and I praise God for setting me free. I thank God for, as I mentioned, my grandma and for putting one lady in my path, Lillian, that helped me when she didn't realize she helped me. It's so important to be transparent and do not mind giving your testimony because you never know who you are helping by doing so. God is truly amazing. He is a present help in time of need. He will have you be at the right place, at the right time, for receiving the breakthrough you need. You must be obedient and go where He leads.

Rhythm 14

Freedom

I know now what it feels like to be free
I am no longer bound to the burdens that once contained me
I have learned to be true to my heart
And confess those things that broke my heart
I have tasted the sweetness of freedom
My soul rest in such peace
To all the things that brought many tears
So earnestly I prayed, that the pain would just go away
Then one day I began speaking what was on my heart
In an instant the burden departed
The yoke was released from me
At last my heart is free!

Stage Exit

Never be afraid of the unknown because God knows all. He will comfort you in your darkest hours. In a song titled "You Just Don't Want to Know" by Pastor Marvin Winans, part of the lyrics says, "Now it's true that God is always there, He said He'd never leave. But at times the human touch is what I need." That human touch came in the way of Lillian's testimony.

Imagine This!

You entered your home after a long exhausting day at work. After winding down from the day's activities, you prepared a delicious dinner and then ate. Next, you took a refreshing shower and prepared for bed. But before deciding to shut down for the night, you decided to watch TV. You chose a couple of sitcoms and then a movie. After watching your favorite shows, you surfed the channels to see if there was anything else on you would like to watch; finding nothing worth watching, you decided to go to sleep, being certain to set your alarm clock for work the next morning. Not more than five minutes after your head hit the pillow, you were sound asleep.

Suddenly, you were woken by the loudest noise you have ever heard in your life. Someone was in your home and was going through the place like a whirlwind. You jumped out of bed to see your home destroyed, realizing a thief had gotten in but was now gone. You looked out your window to see total darkness—no streetlights, no starlight, no moonlight, total darkness. You heard no sound of another living creature. You realized you are all alone. You started to wonder, "What in heavens name just happened!" Then it hit you.

Heaven just happened and what you thought was a thief that whirled through your home was Jesus coming to take you with Him, but you were not prepared, and He didn't have time to wait. Now you have been left behind. Suddenly you heard another loud noise. You opened your eyes and looked over at the alarm clock on your nightstand. It's 6:30 a.m., time to get up and prepare for work.

How will you live your life from this day forward after the night you just experienced?

> For yourselves know perfectly that the day of the Lord so cometh as a thief in the night. (1 Thessalonians 5:2)

> But the day of the Lord will come as a thief in the night; in which the heavens shall pass away with a great noise, and the elements shall melt with fervent heat, the earth also and the works that are therein shall be burned up. (2 Peter 3:10)

> Remember therefore how thou hast received and heard, and hold fast, and repent. If therefore thou shalt not watch, I will come on thee as a thief, and thou shalt not know what hour I will come upon thee. (Revelations 3:3)

> Behold, I come as a thief. Blessed is he that watcheth, and keepeth his garments, lest he walk naked, and they see his shame. (Revelation 16:15)

Backdrop 15

In a world filled with tragedy, so many have lost hope. We may even question whether God really cares. Well, I'm here to say, yes, God cares. He sits high and looks low. It is not God's will that we suffer. He sees all we go through, and still His word promises hope. Jeremiah 29:11 says, "For I know the plans I have for you" declares the Lord plans to prosper you and not to harm you, plans to give you hope and a future.

Rhythm 15

Hope

Have hope for what you believe in
Although you cannot see it
The desires of your heart are granted
Even when you cannot perceive it
Have hope for what you believe in
Although you cannot see it
Build hope on the invisible
Persevere to reach the impeccable
Character falls into place
Having been justified by faith
Have hope for what you believe in
Although you cannot see it
Things that seem impossible
Through hope, they are made infallible
Have hope for what you believe in
Although you cannot see it
Creation subjected to hopelessness
To build in you, hopefulness
Believe in what's not seen
For you were saved in hope and redeemed
Have hope for what you believe in
Although you cannot see it

Through the wonders of God's grace
Know that hope will never fail

Stage Exit

As we exit this stage and the curtains fall, we need hope in a dying world. Be as a little child: believe and hold fast to hope and to your dream(s). Jesus said, "Suffer little children, and forbid them not, to come unto me for such is the kingdom of heaven." Children of God, believe!

Backdrop 16

Have you ever dread doing something and the closer it came to doing that certain thing, your heart started beating a thousand beats per minute? Or you got this big lump in your throat? Or a big knot in your chest? Well, what we have dread doing doesn't compare to what Jesus went through just a few hours before going to the cross.

Rhythm 16

Gethsemane

Imagine if you can when it came upon the day
Jesus our Lord and Savior laid His life away
In the garden of Gethsemane
His soul was sorrowful unto death
For in the coming hours He would face a gruesome test
He would drink of a bitter cup to save a world from sin
The purpose of Jesus's life was to gain life in the end
And of His twelve disciples He called on only three,
Simon Peter, and the sons of Zebedee
Watch here with me while I pray, stay here with me for just this day
And He prayed to His Father concerning the coming hour
To be spare of tribulation that was set for Him to Follow
And returning to the three He found them all asleep
Falling to his knees, he sent up his pleas, three times he asks the
    Father to stop the things to follow, earnestly he prayed, that he
    would be saved, until drops of sweat as blood, fell from his face.
The things that were to come, would separate the Son, from the pre-
    cious heavenly Father after the final hour.
Returning to the three, he found them still asleep
And He bore the cross alone to give the saved an eternal home

Stage Exit

We exit this stage with these final words. The song writer asks a question then provides an answer. "Must Jesus bear the cross alone and all the world go free? No, there is a cross for everyone and there's a cross for me." This is true; we all have a cross to bear. The question is are we willing to take up that cross and follow Jesus?

> Then Jesus said to his disciples, "Whoever wants to be my disciple must deny themselves and take up their cross and follow me." (Matthew 16:24)

The Unexpected

We all have faced the loss of loved ones and the pain seems like more than we can bear. There are times when death can be so tragic that it shakes the very foundation on which we stand. In 2007, my family experienced the loss of Neekie: daughter, wife, mother, granddaughter, sister, niece, cousin, aunt, and a friend.

Then there are times when we pray for a loved one's healing, but still, that special person goes home to glory. Second Corinthians 5:7 says, "For we walk by faith and not by sight." In 2011, a family member was lost to breast cancer. Angie was the picture of faith. If ever you wanted to see the epitome of faith, all you all to do was spend time with Angie. I was with Angie prior to her last trip to the hospital. As she sat on her bed, I helped her get ready. The last words I remember her saying comes from 2 Corinthians 12:9. She said, "God told me, 'My grace is sufficient for you.'"

During such times, we may wonder where God is and does He care. God is always there if we welcome His spirit in our lives. And yes, He cares. John 14:16 says, "And I will ask the Father, and He will give you another advocate to help you and be with you forever."

Take this pain you face one day at a time. The Bible says, "With the Lord a day is like a thousand years, and a thousand years are like a day" (2 Peter 3:8). And even if one day at a time gets to be too much, take it second by second, then minute by minute, hour by hour, then day by day. Days will become months; months will become years; and you will get to a point where you can remember, and you will be able to smile. Revelation 21:4 says, "He will wipe every tear from their eyes. There will be no more death or mourning or crying or pain, for the old order of things has passed away." You may say, "This passage in Revelation speaks of the vision John saw of a new heaven and a new earth. How will this help with what I'm going through now?" Well, I'm glad you ask that question. Matthew 18:18 says whatever we bind on earth will be bound in heaven and whatever we lose on earth will be lose in heaven. When we bind (not let it overpower us) our confusion and heartache on earth, God will bind it in heaven. When we lose things on earth (unforgiveness, anger, or bitterness), God lose it in heaven, thus bringing forth our blessings. Cast your cares on God for he cares for you (1 Peter 5:7).

A Special Rhythm for the Unexpected

I find myself looking for you in the crowd. That look, that face, that smile. Ever since the day you went away, there's been this big empty space. Your exit was brave, I must say; to know you wouldn't see another day on this earth with the people you love, but I know you felt God's tug.

The ones left behind can't explain why you left, leaving so much pain. Don't get us wrong; we know it wasn't your fault. I believe if you had the choice, as Hezekiah did, you would have counted the lost and ask God to allow you to stay, for just a little while longer, maybe a day.

For a day to You, God, is as a thousand years. Using that thought, it would give many more years to hold and be held by the ones we love because you are the epitome of love.

And we know now that heaven is your home. You are with God now; all your pain is gone. And if we had the choice, we would say, "Stay with God. I'll see you another day."

Dedicated to Samantha Harry Brayboy and Angela Harry Gee, gone but never forgotten.

Backdrop 17

Many artists have drawn their view of Jesus on the cross. And if you only look at the version the world draws, you will think, "This doesn't look so bad." Psalm 22 is all about the crucifixion. It is so important to not just read but study and meditate on God's Word. Don't rely on someone else to tell you what the Bible says. I can recall being at a revival where the minister demonstrated what happened to Jesus as he was hung on the cross. The world won't tell the true story, but God's Word will. Nails were placed in the center of Jesus's wrist and not the palm of His hand. And nails were not placed in the center of His feet but the center of His ankle. During this time, when people were nailed to the cross, they were not nailed in what would be called a steady position. What this means is while stretched out on the cross, the body kept slouching downward. Taking a breath was difficult, and the victim would then have to continuously lift themselves back up to breathe, which cause excruciating pain. Understanding what truly happens during a crucifixion is vital to understanding the sacrifice Jesus made for our salvation.

Rhythm 17

The True Me

Man's pictures are not realization of the things that were done to me. The man you see on the cross does not begin to depict the real image of me. For if they drew the truth of what was done to me, you would've shuddered to witness the true crucifixion of me. Everything the world has shown you seems glamorous to me but the pain and agony I endured that you will never see. So allow me to explain exactly what happened to me.

It all began one Friday night in a garden called Gethsemane. My Father had already told me of things that were to be, and to be honest, I had second thoughts because sin never befell me. I prayed to My Father in Heaven, three times was my endeavor, to remove from me this cup. I wish not to go through such stuff. But of course, I will do My Father's will; it's my purpose in life; that's why I was sent here.

Of my twelve disciples, there was one who betrayed me. He beaconed my enemies with a sign, the kiss of death, you see. As they laid hold of Me, I replied, "There was no need to betray me. I preached in your synagogues day and night. Why didn't you then arrest me?" As they led me away, there was much I could have said, but My Father in Heaven watched over Me, so I held my peace instead. The high priest asked of me, was I the One said to be, the begotten Son of God, the One to live for eternity. I responded to him, "I Am, and you shall see me seated at the right hand of the power and glory of God. It is I whom He has called."

He said my words were blasphemy, and for that, he convicted me; I was sentenced to die on the cross to pay an expensive cost, for a debt I never owed to save humanity from the foe. Then the beatings began, a multitude of soldiers slapping one man. Their mission was to shame me; they stripped me, so all could see my naked body that bleed; they didn't realize I was led. To the point I came to stand, all this done by God's hand. As they spat in my face, there was no shame nor disgrace. And that was just the beginning of the pain I endured from the enemy; my body they badly beat until even I could see my bones that were once covered, flesh hung off. I cried to my Father in heaven. The crowd began to mock me because they could plainly see the one who preached of God's great love was nailed to the cross like a lowly thug.

My strength I no longer had. My broken body continuously bled. And when all was said and done, I, being the true and begotten Son, gave up the ghost and died with only God by my side. Then there was one who came of tradition to break my legs, but seeing I was dead, he pierced my side instead, and when the blood was no longer in my veins, the water or baptism came. So they laid me in a tomb, thinking my life was doomed; they placed guards at my grave, which was foolish being they thought I was dead. I descended to the lower parts of earth. I must admit that hurt because I was separated from the Father, the One who holds all power. I ascended to the high place of heaven and is seated at the right hand forever. Look not to the image of man's cross for I am risen and has paid the cost, the deadly cost of your sins, and this is how your salvation begins.

Stage Exit

We exit this stage with a lot to be said. Bishop Davis preached a series once titled "Cults, Occults and Isms." The series placed light in so many dark places of the Christian walk. One thing I remember him saying in these teachings was this: "Stop looking at Jesus nailed to the cross. He is risen and no longer on the cross!" A sermon by

Bishop T.D. Jakes states, "We are looking for Jesus where he no longer is." This even supports Bishop Davis's statement.

The Bible tells of how Mary and the others went to the tomb looking for Jesus after he foretold he would rise on the third day. We continue to look to Jesus on the cross. Now, don't hear what I am not saying, as my friend Chris Gee would say. I am not lowering the significance of Jesus being nailed to the cross. The glorious part is that the cross was not the end.

Backdrop 18

More times than not, I find myself allowing my flesh to overpower my spirit. Referencing back to Genesis 1:26, when God created our spirits, He created it (our spirit) like Him. "Let us the Father, the son and the holy spirit make man in our image." God's plan was for us to be led by our spirits, which is like His spirit and not by our flesh (our vessels of time). The Bible tells us how to be led by the Spirit.

> But I say, walk by the Spirit and you will not gratify the desires of the flesh. (Galatians 5:16)

> And your ears shall hear a word behind you, saying, "This is the way, walk in it," when you turn to the right or when you turn to the left." (Isaiah 30:21)

Now what had happened was I didn't listen to any of those scriptures but did my own thing. May I be honest? Sometimes, people get to you so bad that you want to do a Bernie Mac and "bust somebody's head to the white meat." Or do a Madea and "punch somebody in the throat." I never did those things, but it doesn't mean I wasn't thinking it. God is good! Keep reading.

Rhythm 18

One Minute

One minute took it all away
Everything God had to say
He showed me things in me, and He told me how it should be
How I can live my life, without guilt, anger, or strife
He wrote it in a book and told me to take a look
And I did all that He had said but found myself angry and scared
Because I experienced His word to be true
"Satan desires to kill you"
I thought it was hidden in my heart
A place where it will never part
But I felt His word drift away, all in a minute of one day
So how do I get it back? Who will tell me how to do that?
I guess I'll go to the book and take another look
But this time I'll take the time to pray
So that His word will not stray
From the deepest part of my heart, that's where God said it will not
    part
Now I know that it's a battle: You know keeping Satan out of the
    saddle
But God said the battle is His, letting me know, Satan doesn't rule
    here (in my heart).

So why in a minute of one day, I let that old serpent take it away?
It's because while reading the book, I took my eyes off the Creator
of the book
Became wrapped up in the stories of the book instead of the message
in the book
I must keep my eyes stayed on Jesus. And resist that old creator of evil
So, the next time he comes my way
God's word won't vanish in a minute of one day.

Stage Exit

My pastor, Vincent Riley, has a saying: "Represent Jesus well."

On Broken Pieces

And the soldiers' plan was to kill the prisoners, lest any of them should swim away and escape. But the centurion, wanting to save Paul, kept them from their purpose, and commanded that those who could swim should jump overboard first and get to land, and the rest, some on boards and some on parts of the ship. And so, it was that they all escaped safely to land.

—Acts 27:42–44, NKJV

Sometimes our lives seem broken, and we start to believe that whatever we are going through, it's never going to change. We begin accepting the situation for what it currently is and lose hope. We face storms in our lives, and we brace ourselves for the worst and rarely have a plan for survival. Our mentality is, "This is the way it is, this is the way it will be, so I may as well get used to it."

Paul and the other passengers realized the storm wasn't the end and, in an effort, to prove it wasn't the end, they held on to whatever they could and made it to dry grounds. Acts 27:22 says, "And now I exhort you to be of good cheer, for there shall be no loss of any man's life among you, but of the ship only." I don't know what broken piece you must hold on to for riding out the storm. Maybe it's a sermon you heard, or maybe it was an encouraging word; maybe it's a memory. Whatever that broken piece or broken pieces are, hold on; the storm won't last always. And God promised, you will make it to safe grounds.

Backdrop 19

Most of my friends and associates are women. As I engage in and listen to the conversation, we are frustrated because of failed relationships or have faced disappointments. We are, at times, giving what isn't being given back to us, and sometimes we are lonely. We have looked for love in too many places and some wrong places. Thinking about the heart of my sisters, I was led to write the following poem:

Rhythm 19

For My Sisters

My sisters are many, Lord, and in need of your hand
We stand at the gate of uncertainty because we sometimes don't
    understand
We feel as though we're all alone when things go astray
We need your love and assurance that You will lead the way
We often get away from You because life problems seem so grand
I pray, Father, You will comfort us when we feel we're at wit's end
I do not understand, God, the trials we sometimes go through
We seek your face for answers, Lord, to show us what to do
I know it's in your word, God, the route that we must take
Sometimes doubt get in our way and that's when we say:
"Where are you, Father? I thought You were here to stay
I feel adversity around me, I feel there's no better way."
That's when Your spirit says, "Believe in Me, trust in Me, spend time
    Me, obey Me,
Follow Me, worship Me, put no other god before Me
I'll hear your prayers. I'll heal your despairs
I've already shown you how much I care
Let go of your hurt, let go of your pain
Give your burdens to Me, I still answers prayers."

Stage Exit

We will exit the stage with my life experience. There have been many nights I cried myself to sleep: worried, hurt, and angry. One night as I prayed, I asked God how I can trust this person I continue to allow myself to lose peace and joy over? God replied, "All you need to do is trust Me."

Backdrop 20

There is a saying that goes "You don't know my story." So true. We may think we know what a person is going through or has gone through, but as the quote goes, "Until you have walked a mile in my shoes, don't judge me." Sometimes Christians can be the most critical. "Well, it doesn't take all that." Second Samuel 6:16 tells of how David danced before the Lord and how his wife despised him in her heart for doing so.

Rhythm 20

My Tears

My tears are not for your observation
To check me out to see why they fall
For you know not whence I come
And you have not realized the glory of God's call
Do not watch me as though I'm a showpiece
Because the Spirit of the Lord is upon me
He is the rock of my salvation
He is the deliverer of my soul
My tears are not for your entertainment
To go and tell someone what you saw
To discuss me in your "fellowship groups"
Nor to evaluate me to see when I fall
My tears are a way of cleansing me,
My tears are a way of soothing me,
My tears are a way of God forgiving me,
My tears are for the glory of God upon me.
He understands my walk and the trials that I've been through
He sees what's inside my heart, something people can never do.

Stage Exit

Many curtain calls took place before we were able to exit this stage. God created us with emotions and with displaying those emotions; tears fall. We should never judge how a person reacts to certain things, as in to say, "It doesn't take all of that."

When I was about ten years old, my cousin Joyce died. She had been sick for a long time. My grandmother, Mattie, took care of Joyce from the moment she became sick until the day she breathed her last breath. I will always remember what the pastor said that delivered the eulogy. He looked at my grandmother and said, "Here sits Mattie, Joyce's grandmother, who has not a tear to shed because she knows she did everything she could for Joyce while she was on this earth."

Now, that statement wasn't to condemn my grandmother because she wasn't crying as many of us were. But it was to honor her for the dedication she gave to caring for a granddaughter until her death. It was a statement that said, "Mattie has no regrets because she gave all her love while she (Joyce) was here."

Some emotions come with tears and some don't. I know at some point my grandmother cried. Not only for the loss of her first grandchild but for the great-grand LaKita (age five at that time) whose mother is now gone and whom she never really got a chance to know. Put away judgmental thoughts and glares; you don't know their story.

Worse before Better

(Matthew 24:1–31)

What do you do when life gets worse before it gets better? Read Exodus 5; it gives an account of life getting worse before it got better for the Israelites. God had instructed Moses to go to Pharaoh and tell him, "Let my people go." As a result, the Israelites were not allowed to go, and to make matters worse, their workload increased.

The Israelites were in bondage to Pharaoh for hundreds of years. God saw the injustice they were facing, and He heard their cries (Exodus 3:7). God sent Moses to Pharaoh to command him to let His people go. With Moses going to Pharaoh, the Israelites paid the price, and they cried out again. This time, their cries were not to God but to Pharaoh and the task masters. They began pleading with the task masters to lessen the workload or to at least go back to the way things were when they received assistance with a portion of the daily duty required.

I heard a sermon by Pastor Joel Osteen one day that brought out an interesting yet sad point. The cries of the Israelites begged for the workload to be lightened so that they could complete the given task for that day. Pastor Joel pointed out this, "They were praying to be better slaves." They were not praying for the work to stop all together but to be lightened. When I heard that, it was as if an alarm started going off. Often, things will get worse before they get better. When

99

we have a mind-set of "This is how it will always be," "I will always be broke," "I will always be sick," or "I will always be in a dead-end job," we are basically committing ourselves to remain in bondage.

Instead of climbing up the rough side of the mountain, Jesus said in Mark 11:23, "Truly I tell you if anyone says to this mountain, go throw yourself into the sea and does not doubt in their heart but believe that what they say will happen it will be done for them." No disrespect to this Gospel favorite, but instead of climbing the rough side of the mountain, command that it move out of the way!

Backdrop 21

John 8:4–5 says, "'Teacher,' they said to Jesus, 'this woman was caught in the act of adultery.'" I always wondered how she was caught in the act of adultery. I'm certain this act wasn't done in a public place. Were the ones that caught her in the act hiding in the bushes waiting outside her house or the house of the man? Were they in the hotel room next door with their ears pressed against the wall? And another thing, one must wonder where was the man she was caught with in the very act? Why wasn't he brought before Jesus and the crowd?

They go on to say, "the law of Moses says to stone her. What do you say?" Jesus didn't answer but stooped down and began writing something in the sand. They kept demanding an answer. Jesus stood up and said, "Let he who is without sin cast the first stone." He stooped down and wrote in the sand again.

The Bible doesn't give an account as to what Jesus wrote in the sand, but as Bishop Davis would say, "If I can use my sanctified imagination, I would say he began to write the sin of each man that brought the woman before him." And one by one, as they read what Jesus wrote about them, they walked away.

Rhythm 21

A Nation of People

To every life there comes heartache, adversity, and strife
And to each that admits his wrong there comes repentance, courage,
    and storms
To tell one person "I'm sorry" may sometimes be hard to do but to
    stand before a nation there must be God in you
To every soul may come unforgiveness for mistakes unfold?
But if the truth be told we all have issues of our own
So, to a nation of people that's angry, bitter, and cold
Let he who is without sin cast the first stone.

Stage Exit

Well, we are on a stage, and what happens on stage? Dramatization. Here comes that "sanctified imagination" again. I imagine the following is what Jesus wrote:

Obashea—You were with her Monday night. He read it and walked away.

Dasadan—You were with her last Friday night. He read it and walked away.

Abakan—You told your wife and children you were going to Wednesday night prayer meeting. Not! You were with her too. He read it and walked away.

Sin is sin; there is no big sin nor small sin. Cease placing self on a pedestal by saying, "What I do is not nearly as bad as what you do" or "I've never done that." If what is done goes against God's Word, then it's sin.

"All I do is _____." No, no. No buts!

Backdrop 22

Ephesians 5:22–32 uses a metaphor of Christ being married to the church as a husband is married to his wife. The verses speak of how Christ loves the church and how He is the head of the church. And it tells how the church is subject to Christ. Just as Christ is married to (dedicated) the church, we should dedicate ourselves to Christ.

Rhythm 22

Matrimony to Christ

When I'm sick in my spirit and problems plague my soul
I seek the face of Jesus Christ for comfort and control
Hardship will arise the Bible tells me so
But Jesus intercedes for me; only to Him will I go
I search for so many answers in so many wrong places
I forget the One that died and rose to save me from damnation
I will connect myself with Jesus in all I do and say
I will follow His instructions; the Bible shows the way
I will be faithful in the word of God in sickness and in health
I will commit myself to Jesus Christ for the rest of my life.

Stage Exit

Before this backdrop falls, if we have not done so, let's commit ourselves in matrimony to Christ. A marriage is sacred and was designed for eternity. We do understand that an earthly marriage may end for various reasons, but a marriage to Jesus Christ will never end.

Whose Power Is It Anyway?

I'm going to tell you something of which I must admit I am guilty of. There are many things in life we try to change. Sometimes, change is within our power, and sometimes, it's not. My struggle comes with trying to change things that are not within my own power. When we try to change things we have no power over, it leaves us by our own choice, powerless. My situation was like a brick wall I continuously chose to run into. Juanita Bynum made a song where some of the lyrics says, "Never allow anything to have more power over you than the power of the living God." I'm afraid, I did just the opposite. I allowed what I have no control over to control me. I was like the Israelites, wondering in the wilderness of too many years. It's not easy to get out, but through God, it's possible. All things are possible with God's hands on it if we take our hands off it.

Backdrop 23

We put a lot of time and effort in the upkeep of our outer body. For instance, we get nice hair duos and haircuts, manicures, and pedicures, tans and plastic surgery, exercising and bodybuilding. And the list goes on and on. But what about that which will live on forever? We feed our earthly bodies every day, but how often are we feeding our spirits and our souls?

There is an old Cherokee legend about the war raging inside of man. A Cherokee grandfather tells the story to his grandson. You can visit http://www.firstpeople.us/FP-Html-Legends/TwoWolves-Cherokee.html for the full story. "There are two wolves fighting inside of us," he tells the grandson. "One is evil, and one is good." The grandson asks, "Which one will win, Grandfather?" The grandfather replied, "The one you feed."

Food provides nourishment and strength. When we don't feed our physical bodies, it gets weak. Well, the same principle applies to our spiritual bodies. If we are not feeding the spirit and the soul, it gets weak. Second Corinthians 10:4–5 says, "For the weapons of our warfare are not carnal but mighty in God for pulling down strongholds, casting down arguments and every high thing that exalts itself against the knowledge of God, bringing every thought into captivity to the obedience of Christ." And Ephesians 6:12 says, "For our struggle is not against flesh and blood, but against the rulers, against the powers, against the world forces of this darkness, against the spiritual forces of wickedness in the heavenly places." With that being said, you can't fight spirit with flesh.

You fight spirit with spirit, and the rulers of dark places are of spirit, and if we are to prevail, we must be strong in spirit.

Rhythm 23

My Spirit, My Soul

I must feed into my spirit, feed into my soul
The true and living Word of God
So my temple will grow strong
I must feed life into my surroundings, feed life into my home
The spirit of the Lord Jesus must consume me
Body and soul
It must be embedded in my spirit, embedded in my soul
Shut up in my body
Just like fire in my bones
It must flow throughout my spirit, flow throughout my soul
Just as the blood runs warm through my veins
Keeping my temple from growing cold
I will accept life into my spirit
I will accept life into my soul
I will accept it in the name of Jesus, my comforter, and my Lord.

Stage Exit

We exit the stage with this thought: what we say, do, listen to, watch, and where we go has an effect on our spirit. The enemy has tricked so many into believing it doesn't hurt to watch certain TV shows or movies. We often say, "Aww, one show won't hurt. One look, one drink, one smoke, one time won't hurt." Allow me to leave you with this. Dr. Charles Stanley address that very excuse: "One won't hurt." He said, "All it took was one bite and it destroyed everything."

> But the Lord God warned him, "You may freely eat the fruit of every tree in the garden—except the tree of the knowledge of good and evil. If you eat its fruit, you are sure to die." (Genesis 2:15–17, NLT)

> The woman was convinced. She saw that the tree was beautiful, and its fruit looked delicious, and she wanted the wisdom it would give her. So, she took some of the fruit and ate it. Then she gave some to her husband, who was with her, and he ate it, too. (Genesis 3:6)

One bite was all it took to change mankind.

Backdrop 24

If we are not careful, we will live our lives with a defeated mind-set. The Bible is filled with the promises of God. Deuteronomy 20:4 says, "For the Lord your God is the one who goes with you to fight for you against your enemies to give you victory." Not all promises are seen immediately, but we must stand firm on them and not give up.

Rhythm 24

A Place of Victory

A place of victory, this is my cry
I stomp on defeat and its attempt to bring me down
I hear shouts of God's promises echoing from high grounds
Standing firm on His word unshaken, undisturbed
If I listen to my surroundings, I hear give up
If I focus on the tangible, it declares you are broke
If I see what's in front of me, I have mountains to climb
A small mustard is planted in the ground
A place of victory is where I stand
All other ground is sinking sand
The deceiver tries to put my faith to the test
A place of victory is where I rest.

Stage Exit

Romans 4:17 says, "Call those things that be not, as though they were." We must claim the victory even before we see it.

Open Wounds

While preparing dinner one day, I accidently cut my index finger. The cut was deep, and I ended up in the ER. I had to get six stitches to close the wound. I left the ER with my finger warped in gauze and was told to keep the finger bandaged for seven days. After which, I was to return to have the stitches removed and I could then have full use of my finger again.

During the seven days, I guarded my finger as if it was the golden finger. On the seventh day, I went to my primary doctor to have the stitches removed. He placed three small strips over the wound, advising this was extra protection just in case the wound reopened. He also advised the strips will fall off in a day or so, but other than that, everything looked good.

As I stated earlier, during the seven days my finger was bandaged, I had limited use of it. But a lesson learned for me was what happened after the bandage was off, I still functioned as if the bandage was on my finger. It really amazed me how I allowed a seven-day setback to define how I functioned going forward. Before the cut, my index finger performed great! But for seven days, I had to make minor adjustments until the finger healed; however, my mind-set was trying to make a temporary situation my way of life. The wound was closed, the finger was healed, and the bandage was off; yet, I was afraid to use my finger as I had done thousands of times before the accident.

John 20:19–29 (NLT) tells of how Jesus appeared to His disciples after His resurrection. The only disciple that wasn't there at that time was Thomas. When the others told Thomas the news with excitement, he doubted and said, "I won't believe it unless I see the nail *wounds* in his hands, put my fingers into them and place my hand into the *wound* in his side."

Eight days later, Jesus appeared to the disciples, including Thomas. Knowing Thomas's thought, Jesus went directly to Thomas and told him, "Put your finger here, and look at my hands. Put your hand into the *wound* in my side. Don't be faithless any longer. Believe!"

Lesson learned: we have setbacks in life. We are wounded, broken, and scared, but God can close all wounds, repair anything broken, and see the beauty in our scars. The problem comes when we operate as though we are still wounded. Each time I look at my finger, I see the scar, and I will always see the scar, but guess what? Jesus can still see His scars as well. It's a reminder of the sacrifice He made to save a dying world. It reminds us of the cross, burial, and resurrection. Just as the doctor in the ER stitched up my wound, Jesus will do the same for our spiritual wounds. What He did at Calvary stitched up all our hurts, shame, pains, and disappointments. Some wounds are self-inflicted, and some aren't. Nevertheless, Jesus can heal them all.

The past few years of my life was an open wound. The longer I allowed that wound to remain open, the more contaminates that got in it. The more contaminates that got in, the more the wound hurt. But God showed me through my physical finger wound that just as I seek help to treat and close it up, if I seek Him, He will treat and close my wounded heart. As Jesus told Thomas "Believe!" a lot of times, we must "call those things that be not as though they were" (Romans 4:17, KJV).

Make this the positive power of persuasion. If you think about it enough, imagine it enough, eventually you will convince yourself that you are healed, thus, changing your mind-set.

Once you change the mind-set (because the battle begins in the mind), you can change your outlook and the situation and begin to truly allow God to close the wound forever!

Backdrop 25

In the world of call center quality assurance, there is a practice we have called inadvertently interrupting. If the Customer Service Representative (CSR) is speaking and the customer begins to speak over the CSR, the CSR must stop speaking immediately. If he/she continues to speak to get their point across, quality assurance will take points away from the overall score for inadvertently interrupting. When we hear the word *interrupt*, we think of rudeness, disrespect, or out of place. But I have found a positive side to some interruptions.

Rhythm 25

Jesus Interrupted
(Inspired by Minister Sylvia Foster)

Jesus interrupted death by fire for three Hebrew boys who refused the king's desires. They refused to bow down; they refused to eat; they refused to obey the king's decree. The fire was turned up seven times its norm; the boys were bound; in the furnace they were thrown. The king stood up, astonished to see, three men unbound, how could this be? Walking amid the fiery furnace, a fourth man he saw, the one who has all power (Daniel 3).

Jesus interrupted a little girl's sleep, commanding death to take a back seat. Her time is not yet, her time is not near, casting out doubt, casting out fear. One touch of his hand, her body he healed (Mark 5:35–42).

Jesus interrupted fits of rage, abolished spirits of evil, making them behave (Mark 5:1–19; Mark 9:22).

Jesus interrupted an issue of blood, spoke to its infirmity with compassion and love (Matthew 9:20–22).

Jesus interrupted a blind man's cry, sitting by the road as others passed by. The crowd tried to hush him, but he knew the truth: Jesus, Son of David, was passing through. Jesus asked him, "What do you want me to do?" In essence he said, "that I might see you."

And at that very moment, that exact day and time, Jesus opened blinded eyes (Mark 10:46–52).

Jesus interrupted the stench of death. He called Lazarus by name, not to confuse death. For if he hadn't call death by name, all that laid resting in their grave would've rose up the exact same day.

Stage Exit

Jesus, if you call, will interrupt pain and sorrow, depression and oppression, sickness and disease, emotional and physical abuse—but only if you allow the interruptions.

Backdrop 26

Genesis 1:20–28 tells of God's creation of every creature that lives on the earth. Adam had the responsibility of naming every creature God brought to him, including female. The Bible doesn't confirm this, but my spirit tells me that God already had names for every creature on the face of the earth. Because God created mankind in His image, Adam's spirit was so connected with God's spirit that he named every creature exactly what God had already called them to be.

God caused a deep sleep to come on Adam. He took one of Adam's ribs and formed a helper. Genesis 2:22 says, "Then the rib which the Lord God had taken from man He made into a woman," and He brought her to the man. Verse 23 is the basis of my theory because Adam called the creation presented to him exactly what God had already called her in verse 22: "woman." He didn't say, "She will be called Eve." He said, "She shall be called 'woman.'"

Rhythm 26

Live by the Call
(Inspired by God telling Adam to
name all the creatures He created)

You are made in the image of God
A little lower than the angels above
Having dominion over creatures, big and small
God spoke to your spirit before you were formed
And from earth's substance He molded man
In His likeness and wholeness then gave
To you His breath of life
According to His will, power, and might
Your spirit then aligned with God
The names of life were then called
Every name man spoke was confirmed
Through God's awesome works
You were not called to be oppressed
You were not called to be depressed
You were called a son and daughter of God
Deserving only His best

Stage Exit

We have allowed the unfortunate events of life label us: lack, defeated, sick, or broke. But God calls us a royal priesthood, sons and daughters of the Lord Almighty, heirs of God and coheirs with Christ, a holy nation, God's special possession, just to name a few.

Lead us not into temptation

Remember earlier, I mentioned times I didn't understand what the Word of God meant and seek God for answers? Well, a portion of the Lord's prayer was one that I didn't understand. "Lead us not into temptation." At first glance, one would think (as I did) how is it possible for God to lead us into temptation?

We have read the accounts of Jesus being tempted by Satan. Matthew 4:1 (NLT): "Then Jesus was *led by the Spirit* into the wilderness to be *tempted* there by the devil." To begin with, God led Jesus into the wilderness to be tempted; so if God led Jesus to be tempted, why then does the Lord's prayer states, "Lead us not into temptation?" Hold on to your seat because you are in for a bumpy ride from one scripture to the next.

James 1:13–16 states, "Let no one say when he is tempted, 'I am being tempted by God,' for God cannot be tempted with evil and he himself tempts no one." Sounds like a contradiction, huh?

Well, let's dig into this a little deeper by looking at 1 Corinthians 10:13 (NLT): "The temptations in your life are no different from what others experience. And God is faithful. He will not allow the temptation to be more than you can stand. When you are tempted, he will show you a way out so that you can endure."

Sidebar: there is a lot to be understood here, and for this reason, the Bible says in 2 Timothy 2:15 (KJV), "Study to show yourself approved unto God, a workman that need not to be ashamed, rightly dividing the word of truth."

We must be careful when it comes to fully understanding God's Word. If not, we may be led to believe the Bible contradicts itself.

Rest assured, the Bible is true from beginning to end, and there are no contradictions; you just need to read, study, and understand from one point to the next.

Okay, let's break this down. The Word of God clearly tells us temptations will come our way; there's no way around it. However, God has promised us that there is no temptation that will come our way which He has not given us the power to overcome. Jesus is the perfect example of being tempted and avoiding the temptation. We have the same power!

Remember Job? Satan had to get permission from God to tempt Job. God doesn't lead us into temptation, but He will allow temptation to come our way. Temptation is a test. It tests our faith and our character. The events that occurred in the wilderness when Jesus was tempted by Satan was a test. God sent His only begotten Son to us for several reasons. One was to show us how to live a godly life. And that the same spirit in Him (Jesus) is the same spirit in us. Therefore, if Jesus resists the temptation in the desert, we can resist as well. God gives us a free will. "Choose for yourselves this day whom you will serve" (Joshua 24:15, AMP).

When I first asked God to help me understand, this is what I heard the Spirit say. It was so simple: "Pray to me for everything you have need of, but first, you must make me the desire of your heart. And when you make me the desire of your heart, I will provide for you everything you need. Even something as simple as keeping an old washer and dryer working so that you won't be *tempted* to go in debt to buy a new one. But, if by my power, I keep it running and you go and buy a new washer and dryer, don't say you were tempted by God. Because I provided what you needed, and you went out on your own to get newer or prettier."

God's promises are yes and amen if we make Him the desire of our heart. When we make Him the desire of our hearts, temptation is null and void because we know that whatever we desire (being acceptable unto God), He will give to us.

Ugly Things, Beautiful Places

"Ugly things happen in beautiful places." That was the statement made by Pastor Vincent Riley one Sunday morning. The sermon was based on Acts 3:1–11. It's the story of a man, lame since birth, which is brought to the temple entrance called Beautiful Gate. He sat and begged as people passed by each day. We can guess that because of his condition, this man was not able to support himself. Nothing he did caused him to be lame; it happened at birth.

Life is a beautiful gift from God, but some ugly things happen in this beautiful gift of life. St Jude Hospital is filled with beautiful lives facing an ugly thing called cancer. Sometimes, the ugly things in this beautiful thing called life results in one deciding that taking their very own life is the only way to make it beautiful again. Or there are those who take away the beautiful life of others.

We have people facing poverty, abuse of all kinds, loneliness, loss of loved ones, or divorce, just to name a few. And if we are honest, we sometimes have ugly attitudes and words coming from beautiful bodies.

Let's revisit Acts 3:1–11. This lame man laid at the gate called Beautiful, suffering. Peter and John comes along and revives this man's beautiful life.

> Then Peter said, "Silver or gold I do not have, but what I do have I give you. In the name of Jesus Christ of Nazareth, rise up and walk." (Acts 3:6)

The beauty of Jesus Christ covers all ugliness. This man was instantly healed. He jumped up and begin praising the name of Jesus.

Ugly things happen in beautiful places, and it's sometimes hard to see the beauty. The important thing to remember is to not allow those ugly things to overpower us. Keep strength on reserve. How is that done, you may ask? It's done by spending time with God. It's done by filling yourself with His Word. So when those ugly places show up, God's beauty will overpower. Also, have trusted loved ones who you are able to confide in. Even when the ugliness shows up, don't be afraid to let others see it. It's my belief, by letting it be seen, it's the only way to wipe it clean. Think of it like this: if you don't see the dirty places, chances are you won't clean it.

Backdrop 27

It bothers me when I hear women answering to demeaning names. What bothers me even more is when women call each other demeaning names. Some answer because they see it as a harmless joke, and some are offended by being called degrading names. Genesis 2:22 called the female spirit "woman," nothing more, nothing less.

Rhythm 27

Woman

Listen, my sisters, to words of truth
Millenniums ago God created you
From the beginning of time you were on God's mind
You were fashioned so carefully from bone of mankind
You were created for a purpose
You were created with a plan
After your existence God presented you to man
One look at your form
One look at your style
One look at your femininity
And I imagine, man smiled
Bone of his bone
Flesh of his flesh
God gave you to man; He gives only His best
So, Woman, you were called, not any other name
Woman, you were called; you were made from man
Woman, you were called; to be a helper to man
Woman, you were called; God has a plan.

ATTENTION WOMEN, FRONT AND CENTER STAGE: we exit with
grace, style, sophistication, intelligence poise, and beauty! We should

never allow others to call us by any name other than what God has called us, which is, woman. We should never call each other by any other name than what God has called us: woman. We should never demean ourselves, other women, nor allow anyone else to disrespect and call us outside of what God has called us: woman.

Backdrop 28

A report from the Centers for Disease Control and Prevention shows the known number of suicides in the United States in 2017, on average was 129 per day. Warning signs are everywhere; it's up to us to recognize them. And of course, we can't be all places all at once, but there is One who is. We must pray without ceasing for those things that we ourselves don't know. How, you may ask, do I pray for something I don't know will happen? You simply pray! We see the world situation, and we are aware of what goes on; we simply pray concerning the things we see.

Rhythm 28

Listen with Your...

One can speak volumes and not utter a word
From the heart flow life's issues of stories untold
Shouts from the mountaintop can linger unheard
A vast empty space in need of God's Word
Not all issues are visible; not all issues make sounds
Be attentive to God's creations to keep the enemy bound
Not all hurts are seen and silence can be heard
Have a discerning spirit to hear unspoken words
Listen with your heart; guard the broken heart
You never know what lives you save
Remain steadfast in all God's ways.

Stage Exit

Sometimes we must listen to what isn't spoken. The saying is so true: "Actions speak louder than words." The Bible says to be sober and vigilant; the devil is seeking whom he can devour.

The enemy has a way of whispering in our ears: "You are nothing, and you will always be nothing. No one loves you. Why are you even here?" Don't listen to the lies of the enemy.

Remember, the enemy hates the people of God. He is jealous that he will never have the promises we have from a loving God. He knows that grace and mercy will never follow him. So his mission is to destroy you because he is destroyed.

Guilty of All Charges

I was inspired to write this passage after listening to a sermon by the late Billy Graham called "Jesus Christ Superstar." At one point, the Reverend Billy Graham talked about three things Jesus was accused of: healing on the Sabbath, befriending sinners, and proclaiming to be the Son of God. I took that statement and expound on it.

There is a popular R&B song by Isaac Hayes called, "I Stand Accused." Then it goes on to say, "Of loving you too much."

Jesus stood accused by Pharisees, Sadducees, Chief and High Priest, and many others on many accounts, even by His disciples at one point. Okay, I know what you are thinking: that's not in the Bible. Well, keep reading and you will see why I believe this.

Jesus was tempted in every situation we are tempted with today. The Bible doesn't specifically give a story or parable to read supporting every temptation, but we know this to be true by reading Hebrews 4:15: "For we do not have a high priest (Jesus) who is unable to empathize with our weaknesses, but we have one who has been tempted in every way, just as we are-yet he did not sin."

Empathy is different from sympathy. Empathy means you have a personal experience with whatever the case is. Sympathy is having compassion for whatever the case is. Hebrews 4:15 clearly lets us know Jesus empathize in cases of temptation, not sympathized. Another scripture supporting Jesus empathize is Hebrews 2:18: "Because he himself suffered when he was tempted, he is able to help those who are being tempted."

At once the spirit sent him out into the wilderness,
and he was in the wilderness forty days, being

> tempted by Satan. He was with the wild animals,
> and angels attended him. (Mark 1:12–13)

Take notice to who led him to the wilderness: God. First Corinthians 10:13 says, "No temptation has overtaken you except what is common to mankind. And God is faithful; he will not let you be tempted beyond what you can bear. But when you are tempted, he will also provide a way out so that you can endure it." We must be discerning of things that come our way which stops us from going through with a plan or a thought. And we must be willing to see what is in our face: the way out.

Jesus was created to be a minister and ministered even from Mary's womb. Luke 1:41 says, "When Elizabeth heard Mary's greeting, the baby leaped in her womb, and Elizabeth was filled with the Holy Spirit." If that's not ministering from the womb, I don't know what is.

God has called every born-again believer to minister, not to say you must have a church and be in a pulpit, but to minister daily. And yes, we must be born again to be ministers for God because the first birth was in iniquity. Psalm 51:5 (NIV) says, "Surely I was sinful at birth, sinful from the time my mother conceived me."

While traveling one day, at the age of twelve years old, Jesus fell behind in the crowd, away from Mary, His mother, and Joseph, his earthly father. He was ministering to the crowd. However, before Jesus went out to fulfill the plan of our heavenly Father, take notice of what God did. He allowed Jesus to be tempted. Another thing to be mindful of, although we were created to be ministers of God, He will not send us to do a job we are not equipped to handle. This means there will be times of testing.

Now, on to the accusations I spoke of earlier. Throughout His ministry, Jesus was accused of healing on the Sabbath guilty. He was accused of keeping company with sinners, guilty, and He was accused of claiming to be the Son of the living God, guilty. And here is a sidebar: He was tempted in every way but fell not into temptation, guilty.

By now, you should know me and know that I use my sanctified imagination a lot. Jesus is God's Word made into flesh. When God created Jesus, He didn't put a wall around Him nor barricade Him to avoid life's situations and temptations.

He created Him as human, just as He created us. He gave Jesus His word, just as He gave us. He told Jesus right from wrong, just as He told us. And He allowed Jesus to make His own choices, just as He did us.

Not only was Jesus accused by the Pharisees, Sadducees, and others, but let's take a look at His hidden, between the line, as well as undercover accusation by none other than His very own disciples...

"What you talkin' 'bout, Willis?"

The account of the woman at the well tells how Jesus sent His disciples to town to buy food. When they returned, I imagined eyebrows were raised based on the following scripture. Jesus had just revealed to the woman at the well, "I Am the Messiah" (John 4:26)!

> Just then his disciples came back. They were shocked to find him talking to a woman, but none of them had the nerve to ask, "What do you want with her?" or "Why are you talking to her?" (John 4:27, NLT)

Come again? What did they mean, "What do you want with her, and why are you talking to her?"

First of all, based on their (the disciples) time with Jesus, why would they think Jesus wanted something from her (other than salvation)? And why would there be a question as to why He was talking with a woman?

Time to put the sanctified imagination to work and put ourselves in the mind-set of the disciples.

Okay, Jesus, we knew something was up when You sent all of us into town to buy food. It doesn't take twelve people to bring back food; two or three of us would've been sufficient. But, all of a sudden, You send all of us to buy food, and You know it's a long walk, round trip. And all of a sudden, we return to find You alone with this woman who obviously is not a good woman. People in these parts get up at the crack of dawn to draw water from the wells, so we can tell no one wants to be around her. Hmm, we wonder why. Most of all, we are still trying to figure out why it took all of us, twelve grown men, every last one of us, to go and buy food. It ain't like we were buying food for the week. We were only buying food to eat for now; but you sent all twelve of us, not one or two but all twelve of us; makes a person wonder.

With reading John 4:27, it is my belief that Jesus (although unspoken) is being accused by His disciples of having fleshly motives for being alone with and talking to this woman.

Jesus was talking to a sinful woman, guilty. But resisted any temptation that may have risen from a woman that had five husbands and currently shacking up with a man.

Yes, Jesus was accused even by those close to Him but was not guilty of their ungodly thoughts. What He was guilty of is this: healing a woman of her sinful past, being friendly with a sinner, and proclaiming, "I Am the Messiah!" Guilty of all charges!

Backdrop 29

Don't be deceived and don't let your guard down. Peter 5:8 says, "Be alert and of sober mind. Your enemy the devil prowls around like a roaring lion looking for someone to devour." (1 Peter 5:8)

Rhythm 29

The battle is real but so is the Lord. The enemy's assignment: kill, steal, and destroy. He roams the earth, seeking whom he can devour; he knows Jesus has all power. No matter your race, no matter your creed, no matter your color, his goal is to succeed. By any means necessary, he will stick to his plan, deceiving the world and destroying man. He doesn't fight fair; his words are snares to trap you into believing God doesn't care. Don't be deceived by what it looks like; God is mighty in battle; He is in the fight. He set the ending at the beginning; He's an all-seeing, all knowing God. The battle is not yours; it is the Lord's.

Stage Exit

Let's visualize this scripture: Revelation 12:7–12. Michael and his angels fighting against the dragon and his angels because they wanted the power that only God has. The dragon lost the battle, and he and his angels were forced out of heaven.

It all began when Lucifer's (Satan) pride deceived him into thinking he could be God and hold all the power, the glory, and the honor. So now, he is very angry and will get revenge on God's people by any means necessary. It's important to know that Michael and his angels are still fighting with the devil and his angels. This is what spiritual warfare is about.

Backdrop 30

How would you feel if the one you thought would be your friend to the end decides to leave? Imagine, this person was your running partner, your road dog, your ride-or-die chick, your buddy, your boy, your girl, but when things got a little hard, they left. When things got complicated, they walked out. They heard and saw things they couldn't understand and comprehend, so they left. Well, this is the account of John 6:53–70. Jesus revealed to His disciples, "Unless you partake of my flesh and blood, you will not have eternal life."

Rhythm 30

Where Shall I Go

And it came a time when Jesus said, "my blood and my flesh is the only way. For everlasting life, you must feed off me. I am God in the flesh; this you shall see. If you abide in me, I will abide in you, it was my Father in heaven that created me for you. To save you from sin, to save you from death, to provide for you an eternal rest."

But this saying of Jesus was hard for many to take. They turned from this walk—a big mistake. Then turning to the twelve, these words Jesus said, "Will you also turn away?" And Simon Peter, recognizing truth, answered the Lord, "Why would we leave you? You are the way, the truth and the life. It is from you we have eternal life."

Stage Exit

Misunderstandings change lives. Something was said, or something was done, and there was confusion or misunderstandings. And for the most part, before we try to clear the matter, we walk away, confused, dismayed, and sometimes lost or angry.

Then some of the disciples misunderstood Jesus's comment, thinking He was literally speaking of eating His flesh and drinking His blood. When in fact, what He meant was, unless we are willing to take up our cross, we will not be able to follow Jesus.

Unless we believe every word that comes from the mouth of Jesus, we can by no means follow Him.

And unless we are willing to believe in the shedding of His blood for the remission of sin and the breaking of His body through crucifixion, we can by no means follow Him.

A Leah Life

Rejection doesn't feel good to anyone. The book of Genesis 29:17 tells the story of Leah who was given to Jacob in marriage. I would imagine a feeling of rejection is what Leah felt. Leah was the daughter of Laban, and she had a younger sister named Rachel. Jacob was in love with Rachel and wanted to marry her. The Bible describes Rachel as being beautiful with a lovely figure but described Leah as being weak eyed or tender eyed. That could make a person feel less than the person being compared to.

Jacob made an agreement with Laban that he would work for him for seven years, free of charge, if, after the seventh year, he could marry Rachel. However, after the seventh year, Laban gave him Leah instead of Rachel as it was tradition that the older daughter should get married first. Jacob was angry that Laban had tricked him. Laban told Jacob that after one week of being married to Leah, he could marry Rachel under the condition he would work seven more years for him; Jacob agreed. The Bible tells how Jacob's love for Rachel was much greater than his love for Leah.

Leah's reality that she was not Jacob's choice must have weighed heavily on her mind and in her heart. The worst thing of all, Leah was being rejected by someone she didn't even ask to be with, but God looked upon Leah with favor. Leah gave Jacob children, but Rachel none for a while. No one asked Leah what she thought, what she wanted, or even how she felt.

She was given to someone who didn't want her and who wasn't in love with her. But God will accept us when others reject us. As a matter of fact, we are God's beloved. He loves us with an everlasting love. And we should love God in return. "For God so loved the world, that He *gave* his only begotten Son, that whoever believes in Him should not perish but have everlasting life" (John 3:16, NKJV).

There, you have it. We don't have to work for His love. We will never receive less love, and He will not reject us. We are beautiful to Him, and He wouldn't change one fiber of our being. Out of the billions of people on the face of the earth, all at one, each of us are His chosen ones. Isn't it amazing that out of billions of people, God chose you?

You may have been rejected by a spouse, boyfriend, girlfriend, friend, coworker, even a mother or father. While listening to Joel Osteen one day, he explained the scripture that says, "Indeed the very hairs of your head are all numbered. Don't be afraid; you are worth more than many sparrows." I never realized that not only are the hairs on our head counted, but they are numbered (Matthew 10:30, NKJV). So, if hair number 1,325 falls out, it will be replaced, but the replacement will not be numbered 1,325. That hair is gone, and another hair will never have that same number as it nor will it be the same. How amazing is that!

After reading this scripture, I was led to study the significance of sparrows in the Bible. Matthew 10:29 (NKJV) says, "Are not two sparrows sold for a penny? And not one of them will fall to the ground apart from your Father." Sparrows were sold by the poorer people of the Bible. And if I could use my imagination, these people were greatly cheated out of what a sparrow was worth. Because they were the poorer citizens, people in the marketplace knew whatever was offered would be accepted. The fact that two sparrows were sold for only a penny shows how little value was placed on sparrows and the people selling them. As with Leah, little value was placed on her. If she had value, her father wouldn't have given her to Jacob as a trade.

You will soon come to learn (if you don't already know) that Jacob was a trickster. I imagine a heated exchange of words took place between Jacob and Laban and that poor Leah heard it all. Think about it, you are the topic of discussion and it's all about how you are not wanted.

The Word of God says, "His eye in on the sparrow, and I know He watches me." We are told not one of them will fall to the ground because He watches. "Look at the birds of the air, for they neither sow nor reap nor gather into barns; yet your heavenly Father feeds them. Are you not of more value than they" (Matthew 6:26–34)?

God created everyone and everything with a purpose. Anything rejected is not needed or wanted. *Merriam-Webster's* definition of rejection is: refuse to accept, refuse to hear, obsolete or to cast off. The hairs on your head has a number; your finger, hand and footprints are like no other. Since God took the time to do all this just for us (put your hand on your chest and say, "He did it just for me"), there is no rejection.

Backdrop 31

In 1996, I gave my life to Christ and committed myself under the leadership of Bishop Philip M. Davis. One year, the church set aside one Sunday for the congregation to give over and beyond normal tides and offerings. There would also be a time of fasting and praying leading up to this special Sunday.

After Bishop Davis made the announcement concerning his heart's desire, God reminded me of Abraham and the sacrifice he was willing to make. Genesis 22 tells the story of how Abraham obeyed God's command to take his son Isaac to another place and offer him as a burnt offering. The Bible doesn't give an account of a conversation between God and Abraham concerning these instructions. Use your imagination. I would guess Abraham had a few questions. Although God didn't give the full details, Abraham must have known he and Isaac would both return because he instructed his servants to wait at a certain place while he and the boy go worship. "We will come back to you," He said.

God will never lead us in the wrong direction. Well, keep reading and continue to see how awesome God is if you will give Him your time. He may ask us to do things we feel are difficult to do, but it all works together for his good and ours (Romans 8:28).

Rhythm 31

One Great Day of Giving (Inspired by the late Bishop Philip M. Davis)

Abraham was a man of faith. And to Abraham, God said one day, "Take thy son, the promised son, to a land far from your home. Abide in a place, which I shall show thee, a sacrificial offering you must give me. I will tell you the offering, which I desire, prepare a place to make a fire. Use thy son, the promised son, as a burnt offering to me, this must be done." And although Abraham loved his son, this offering to God comes second to none.

So Abraham built an altar of wood to lay his son; this must be done. For Abraham knew and he understood there are great blessings ahead for him and his son. And just as Abraham was about to slay, from the windows of heaven, he heard God say, "Touch not thy son, the promised son for you withheld not from me that which you love. You were willing to give me this child you love; for your great giving you shall receive blessings from above."

Stage Exit

Our faith will be tested. God may ask us to give to others that which we hold dear to our heart. Know this: whatever God requires of us, it's not a lost—it's a gain. "Put me to the test and see if I will not open the windows of heaven and pour out a blessing you will not have room enough to receive" (Malachi 3:10).

Backdrop 32

That one great day of giving wasn't all about tides and offering over and above the norm. It was also about fasting and praying as mentioned in backdrop number 31. The following poem was also inspired by Bishop Davis.

Rhythm 32

Fasting and Praying

I don't know what to do; I don't know where to begin, but I heard the words of the man of God, "For forty days there shall be no end."

No end to fasting and praying, no end to break through miracles, no end to families reconciling, no end to the church recognizing.

Recognizing the plots of Satan, recognizing the traps he set, recognizing the devices he use to keep us from God's best.

God's best for our families, God's best for our church, God's best for a nation of people that's fallen prey to the world's lust.

I know now what I must do, I know where I must begin. I simply start with the Word of God to which there is no end.

And whatever holds me back, whatever consumes my time, I will put it away too fast and pray and watch break through miracles go forth from this day.

Stage Exit

I have learned that fasting is not limited to food and drink. We can decide to fast from things that take our time away from God. That could be television, shopping, or playing games. We can fast by saying, instead of watching TV for hours upon hours, "I will spend that time reading my Bible." Giving up anything that takes us away from God could be a form of fasting.

Saving Private Ryan— Live Your Life Worthy

The movie *Saving Private Ryan* is based on World War II. Private James Francis Ryan lost three brothers in the war, and he is the last surviving member of the four. A mission was set to find and save Private Ryan and bring him safely home to his family. The efforts to save him were long and deadly; many soldiers lost their lives. There is a scene toward the end of the movie that I will always remember: Private Ryan was told, *"We would want the person for whom we died to live a life worthy of the life we were giving up."* In other words, many lives were lost saving the life of Private Ryan, and he was encouraged to not allow the lives lost to be in vain.

> And when Jesus had cried out again in a loud voice, he gave up his spirit. (Matthew 27:50, NIV)

> I, therefore, the prisoner of the Lord beseech you to walk worthy of the calling with which you were called. (Ephesians 4:1, NKJV)

> I am naturally anti-slavery. If slavery is not wrong, nothing is wrong. I cannot remember when I did not so think and feel. (Abraham Lincoln)

Abraham Lincoln was shot on April 14, 1865 and died April 15, 1865.

> A man who does not have something for which he is willing to die is not fit to live. (Martin Luther King Jr.)

Martin Luther King Jr. was assassinated April 4, 1968.

John Fitzgerald Kennedy (JFK), in a famous 1963 speech, said, "Black people should be able to shop at the same stores as white people without having to demonstrate in the streets, that they should be able to go to college without a military escort, and that they should be able to vote without fear of violence being taken up against them." President Kennedy was assassinated on November 22, 1963.

Many sacrifices were made for the betterment of our lives. The greatest sacrifice of all is what Jesus Christ did on Calvary. The "Garden of Gethsemane" is an account of what Jesus went through before the cross. And "The True Me" gives an account of what Jesus endured on the cross.

President Abraham Lincoln believed slavery was wrong and went through a lengthy process to get it abolished. As a result, he lost his life.

John F. Kennedy and Martin L. King Jr. both lost their lives fighting for racial justice. We all should, as the quote says in *Saving Private Ryan*, live our lives worthy. Jesus should be our foundation of doing whatever it takes to live a godly life.

Yes, life is hard, but it's no reason to live less than what many others died for to make better. We should always keep a mental picture of Jesus's agonizing journey to the cross. We should always remember John F. Kennedy going against all odds, being a white American, fighting day after day for the rights of black Americans. We should mentally put ourselves in the place of Martin L. King Jr., being stabbed, having water hoses, and dogs turned on him (not to mention many others), daily threats on his life, the lives of his family and supporters.

It is my prayer that my readers will encourage others to "live life worthy of all who died to save it."

Backdrop 33

An autobiography in five short chapters by Portia Nelson:

Chapter 1: I walk down the street. There is a deep hole in the sidewalk.

I fall in. I am lost… I am helpless. It isn't my fault.

It takes forever to find a way out.

Chapter 2: I walk down the same street. There is a deep hole in the sidewalk. I pretend I don't see it. I fall in again. I can't believe I am in the same place. But it isn't my fault. It still takes a long time to get out.

Chapter 3: I walk down the same street. There is a deep hole in the sidewalk. I see it is there. I fall in… It's a habit…but my eyes are open. I know where I am. It is my fault. I get out immediately.

Chapter 4: I walk down the same street. There is a deep hole in the sidewalk. I walk around it.

Chapter 5: I walk down a different street.

Rhythm 33

The Big Hole

It's like a big hole in the ground, one I can't seem to get around. And although it's as plain as day, He keeps putting that hole in my way. You would think I would see it coming. After all, I'm no dummy. So I say, "This time will be different. I will not give into your petition." But somehow you have a way of making that hole seem like a better way, to hide from all that troubles me, an escape plan or so it seems. Now, I'm tired of your same old tricks. I have found someone who got me hip. Someone who took the time to show me, all your ways and all your plays. So now, Satan, God has prepared for me a master plan, one which you cannot withstand, so for a lifetime I'm here to stay. The traps you set are of yesterday; that hole you dug for me belongs to you now. My God has saved me!

Stage Exit

The enemy's assignment is to kill, steal, and destroy. And he is determined to complete it by any means necessary. Beware of his traps; they are always the same.

Backdrop 34

I have been blessed by many sermons delivered by my pastor, Vincent Riley. I want to bring attention to two of them: one titled "From Pain to Promise" and the other, "From Sunday to Monday." While listening to these two sermons, I was inspired to write on both and with doing so, I heard "The in-between."

There is an old cliché that goes, "Stuck between a rock and a hard place." Whenever this is said, we think of something bad. Years ago, I received a new outlook on this old cliché. I saw myself as being between a rock and a hard place. But I heard God say, "Who said being between a rock and a hard place is a bad place to be? It's all how you look at it."

Several scriptures in the Bible calls God the rock of our salvation: Psalm 89:26, 95:1; Deuteronomy 32:15, just to name a few. Jesus told Peter in Matthew 16:18, "Upon this rock I build my church and the gates of hell shall not prevail against it."

Webster's definition of rock is: a solid material; a person who is extremely strong; reliable or hard.

Webster's definition of hard is: solid, firm, and resistant to pressure; not easily broken, bent or pierced.

So looking at it from this perspective, if you are between a rock "Jesus" and a hard place "the character of Jesus," then I would say that's a good place to be. It's all about how you look at it: is the glass half full or half empty?

Rhythm 34

You May Not See It, but God Is Filling the In-Between

Pain to Promise

God feels your hurt; God feels your pain. The result: personal gain. What the devil meant for evil, God will turn around for good; the ways of God can be misunderstood.

I lost my loved one; it wasn't fair.

You may sometimes question, "Does God really care?"

All I feel is pain; where is the gain? A promise I don't see, does God truly love me?

Indeed, He does, for God is love; the trials we face becomes a test. A test is a testimony, not only for you, but to help others continue to push through. God promised to wipe every tear from your eyes; He is near the brokenhearted; He is by your side. So from pain to promise, God will see you through all the disappointments that consumed you.

Sunday to Monday

We go to church; we praise the Lord; we fall to our knees and worship our God; now this is Sunday, next comes Monday. And the test begins from the battle within testing your praise, testing your worship; the enemy is watching to defeat your purpose.

You praised His holy name; you worshipped until the end. Now, that deceiver of the world puts his two cents in "You're not worthy. You're not holy. I control your matrimony to the one you call Christ, to the one you praise day and night, to the one you give all the glory, to the one who knows your story."

You go to church Sunday after Sunday; watch out now, here comes Monday.

Saints of God, I'm here to say, the joy you feel shouldn't go away, from Sunday to Monday. God is the same; put His joy in your heart and praise His holy name.

Stage Exit

As we exit the stage, let's hold fast to the glory we experience on Sunday and carry over into Monday and the following days. Now, remember the fasting? We must continue to fuel our spirits with the Word which will carry us through. Before you know it, we are back to Sunday. And pray for the shepherd of the church to strengthen the man or woman of God that has been placed in your life.

Vision

Without a vision the people perish.

—Proverbs 29:18

Write the vison make it plain.

—Habakkuk 2:2

Without a vison, we tend to not be leaders but followers. Our future begins with a vision. Habakkuk stated to not only have a vision but to write the vision down and make it plain so that there is no mistaking.

Our visions are to be nurtured and even supported at times. Now, be extremely careful who you allow around your vision. Even Jesus had a few selected people He had with Him at certain times. Some people may call this the inner circle. The Transfiguration on the mountain, healing Jarius's daughter, and praying in the garden of Gethsemane, during each of those times, he only had Peter, James, and John. They were a part of what I call Jesus's inner circle. An inner circle includes people that will take the vision and run with you, not take the vision from you and run.

The book of Judges 13–16 tells the story of Samson. Toward the end of his life, Samson was captured by the Philistines. He was bond in chains, and the Philistines gouged his eyes out, taking away his *sight* but not his *vision*. What I feel important to realize here is this: a vision is not fulfilled through one of the five senses. It's not fulfilled through eyes (seeing) but through your mind and your heart.

Samson's hair grew back, and he gained his strength back. Because he still had a mind to pray to God, although he had no sight, he still had his vision. He destroyed more Philistines at the point of death than during his entire life. If you read Judges 13–16, you will see Samson's purpose was to rescue Israel from the Philistines.

> "For I know the plans I have for you," declares the Lord, "plans to prosper you and not to harm you. Plans to give you hope and a future." (Jeremiah 29:11)

Proverbs 29:18 says, "Without a vision, the people perish." Proverbs is the book of wisdom. So having a vision is wisdom. The Bible gives many accounts of Jesus healing people, but healing the blind appears most often. And it was always blind men. God has called the man to be the head of his home, to have a vision for his family, and exemplify a godly life. In this case of blind men, it is my opinion that because they had no sight, it affected their mentality. Therefore, Jesus healed them of sight blindness so they could walk in the way God would have them to go without limitations.

My vision for my life was to one day write a book of poetry. My book turned out to be more than a book of poetry but a book of encouragement as well. I was blinded for many years and stopped visualizing the vision. Whatever your vision is for life, never give up and never stop seeing the vision through your mind and your heart.

Backdrop 35

First Samuel 17 is the story of David and Goliath. David was a shepherd boy that tended to his father's flock. People were being taunted by the Philistines day in and day out. Goliath, called a champion, would come out each day to challenge the people of Israel. He was a giant among the people, and all that saw him were afraid except one shepherd boy named David.

We all know the story of how David took five smooth stones and a sling shoot, aimed, and hit Goliath, bringing him down to the ground. But do we really and truly understand the origin of Goliath's fall?

Pastor Melody Burford made Goliath's fall very clear one day. We know that David put a rock in his sling, whirled it around, hit Goliath, and he fell forward.

> Then David put his hand in his bag and took out
> a stone; and he slung it and struck the Philistine
> in his forehead so that the stone sank into his
> forehead, and he fell on his face to the earth.
> (1 Samuel 17:49)

Our thought process probably says the giant should have fallen backward, but the Bible said he fell forward. Does this seem strange? Well, I never thought of this as being strange.

To be honest, I never gave it any thought at all until one Sunday service. This is what I learned: When David's hit caused Goliath to fall forward and not backward, this means there was a force behind

Goliath that pushed him, causing him to fall forward. This revelation knowledge from Pastor Melody blew my mind. We know that God was with David from the beginning, but what we didn't realize, at least I didn't, was that Goliath's fall was not a normal fall.

Rhythm 35

The Force Behind
(Inspired by Pastor Melody Burford)

With a shepherd's bag by his side and five smooth stones inside, a sling shoot in his hand, this is where the battle began between David, the shepherd boy, and Goliath, the giant. Goliath taunted God's people all day, but this young David came to say, "You come before me with great weapons. I come before you with my God's blessings. And all your men will see, there is a great force with me, one which you can't see, one which covers me, one which no man can withstand. And on this day as you stand, my God will bring you down. Your stature will hit the ground, face first, you shall fall, but this fact most of all, a normal hit would blow you back, but this is an unseen attack. I will hurl my weapon toward you. My God stands behind you, and to the ground you will fall by the hand of God who rules over all. Your taunting from this day will end, and the message I will send, you Philistines are through because of the great force that was behind you."

Stage Exit

God is with us. We are not able to see Him with our physical eyes, but we can see Him in spirit and know that if we allow, He is working in our lives.

Backdrop 36

How far would you go to help a friend in need? Many of us use the word "friend" much too loosely. We must understand that everyone we associate with is not our friend. Yes, it's true. Some people are associates, some coworkers, some enemies, and as my Pastor Riley would say, some are your "frenemies." But not all are friends. Let's get the understanding that a friendship is a relationship, and in relationships, there will be times when we disagree, but "at the end of the day," we are friends. The Bible gives us examples of faithful friends. Read and determine whether you are a friend and whether you have true friends.

Rhythm 36-1

David and Jonathan
(1 Samuel chapters 18-20)

Jonathan was the son of King Saul. After the battle Saul called for David to come and stay, at his home because David slayed Goliath and the Philistine army but after the battle the people honored David instead of Saul; from this point, King Saul began to fall.

His jealousy overtook him, and his plan was to kill him, David, the shepherd boy, but Jonathan knew it all: the plan his father the king had conjured up to kill his friend; so he took David, the Bethlehemite, hid him from the King's sight.

"My father seeks to kill you. For this reason, I must hide you. Stay here in this secret place, and I shall meet my father face-to-facet o speak on your behalf, to convince him your life must last. Truly, you are my friend, soul brothers to the end, and what your heart desires, I shall grant you with all my power. Trust me, your ears and eyes, and if I perceive my father still despise, the man of God as you are, I will send word for you to remain far."

Rhythm 36-2

Job and His Friends
(Job 2:11–13)

Satan roams to and fro, seeking all he can destroy, presenting himself to God one day, to the adversary God did say: "Have you tried my servant Job? He's one of a kind, blameless, and righteous and fears the Lord.

So Satan answered and basically said, "This man you speak of, I should say, he's wealthy and prosperous, well-known in the land, but take all away and he will stray." And since God knows beginning to end, He granted Satan; a challenge begins. And it came one day, to Job, messengers said, "All you have was taken away. Your animals are gone, your children are dead, nothing is left, I regret to say." Then Job arose and tore his clothes, fell to the ground and worshipped the Lord.

Now, Satan still roamed to and fro, seeking all he might destroy, presenting himself to God one day, to the adversary God did say, "Have you tried my servant Job? He's still one of a kind, blameless, and righteous and fears the Lord. Your challenge went forth, and as you see, my servant Job still worships Me."

So Satan replied and in essences said, "Possessions are nothing, but this I say, touch his body, take health away, I guarantee he will stray." God still knows beginning to end and granted Satan once again.

Satan touched the body of Job, inflicting pain from head to sole. His wife being angry, somewhat said, "Curse the Lord and die this day!"

But Job was faithful and answered her plea, "Foolish woman, cease your speech. God give great things but sometimes come bad for the glory of the Lord. I give up all I have."

Hearing of his misfortune, Job's friends arrived, crying when they saw him, brokenhearted inside. For seven days and seven nights, they sat on the ground, no other in sight. They spoke not a word; they comforted Job's soul, dumping dirt on their heads; Job wished he was dead. They chatted, they debated on Job's fate, and in the end, Job prayed for his friends. Job paid a cost; God restored all that was lost. Job rejoiced in the end after interceding for his friends.

Rhythm 36-3

Luke 5:17–20

As Jesus was teaching in the house one day, many people came from far away. Pharisees and Sadducees gathered in the house, checking Jesus out, seeing what He's about. Teaching and healing, as times in the past, the house was crowed, no one could pass through the windows nor through the door; people were desperate to hear from the Lord. And as He was teaching in the house that day, there were men that came from far away. Their friend was sick and wanted to be healed; they looked at the crowd and wondered how they would get their friend to the One who heals; they looked around and probably smiled. A plan they had to help their friend, carried him to the housetop, from there they dropped their friend down to Jesus despite all the people; determined was the goal to help save a soul. And when Jesus saw the faith of the friends, it was at this point He forgave His sins.

Stage Exit

Would you say that you are a friend? Are the people you call friends worthy to be called friend?

The Word of God Is Like

Dear readers,

One thing about me is I tend to find significance in everyday living. A simple jack-in-the-box toy brought to me the following words of encouragement.

The word of God is not packed down in a little box that you turn a side handle and it pops out at you. You wind it up a few times, and then you see or understand the full picture. I should say not. If I had to describe the Word of God, I would say the Word of God *is like* a five thousand or more piece jigsaw puzzle. You see the big picture before you (remember, "The Vision") but it's all in broken pieces (remember, "On Broken Pieces"). You must spend time with the Word of God to make the vision a reality.

You empty all the pieces out; that *is like* opening yourself to God. You pour out the pieces of the puzzle on a table. The pouring out of the pieces *is like* your heart and soul. The table *is like* an altar. You then start to spread the broken pieces out. This *is like* being transparent, no condemnation or shame. Once you spread the pieces out, things start getting clearer because it's not all jumbled together. This *is like* revelation knowledge.

With a puzzle, you must take time putting it together. You sort through the broken pieces. And although broken, they are all a part of the final big picture, and all pieces are needed, each one equally important. No matter how odd the pieces look, they all fit together for one common good; the picture or the vision is how I chose to look at it. This *is like* how God looks at us; although broken into pieces, we are important to Him.

Understanding God's Word takes time. We must be willing to meditate on it day and night. It *is like* food for the body. As it's been said, we feed our physical bodies at least once per day. It is also just as important to feed our spiritual body daily. We have so much technology to help with this.

We can download Bible apps that will send daily scriptures to our phone. We have no excuse for not studying the Word of God; if we don't, it would be *like* giving up your life for a worthless cause.

Backdrop 37

In the past, I worked for a company that sold and shipped Amway products. Some of the items were Christian based. One product I remember clearly was a T-shirt with a slogan on it that said, "Whatever it Takes." I purchased one of those T-shirts and wore it proudly. Whatever it takes to me means determination. For years, I was determined to write a book of poetry. I am also determined to have my poems made into Gospel songs. I watched an interview done with Berry Gordy. Mr. Gordy spoke of Smokey Robinson. He said, "He was a wonderful poet, but he didn't know how to write songs." I believe that I, too, am a wonderful poet but have no knowledge of writing music. I am working diligently on my dream of getting this book published, and if you are reading this, God has made a way for my dream to come true. I also have a dream of being a songwriter— not music, just the lyrics. And I will do "Whatever it Takes" (being acceptable to God) to make my dream a reality.

Rhythm 37-1

Jochebed, the mother of Moses, is an example of, "Whatever it takes."

Exodus 2

There rose a king back in the day,
Pharaoh was his name and this he said:
"Israel is mightier than we will ever be,
make life difficult for them; make them weak."
But what Pharaoh didn't realize, Israel had God on its side,
and they grew the mightier despite Pharaoh's pride.
And once Pharaoh realized Israel grew stronger day by day,
he commanded male babies be thrown away.
Cast them into the river, was Pharaoh's demand to put an end
to Hebrew men.
But Jochebed, one of the Hebrew mothers, for the love of her
son, kept him undercover.
For three months she hid him but there came a day,
she had to let him go so that he might be saved.
Making for him a little haven, placed in the river hoping some-
one will save him.
"Whatever it takes, I can imagine," she said,
"I will save my son from the one who wish him dead."
Moses was his name and he grew up to be
the one that lead the Israelites, helping set them free.

Rhythm 37-2

Jacob is an example of "Whatever it takes" as he wrestled the angel of God.

Genesis 25, 27, and 32

Jacob and Esau were brothers, you see.
Twin boys born, two nations came forth.
Esau, a hunter, a man of the field, was loved by his father who feast on his meals.
Jacob, a swindler, who wheeled and deal, was loved by his mother who encourage he steal;
The birthright given to the eldest son.
Jacob born last of Isaac's two sons.
Jacobs desired to be the first and swindled his brother's rights of birth.
He cooked a stew because he knew his brother was tired; he wouldn't think things through.
Esau was hungry; Jacob was cunning for Esau's birthright with all his might.
So, Esau gave in and in the end gave up his birthright for fleshly delights.
It came a time when Isaac knew, his days were numbered, and earthly life would be through.
He called to Esau, his eldest son, and said to him, "This must be done.

"My soul must bless you and give your birthright before this is done, I ask you, my son.

"Go out to the field and hunt for game, prepare me a meal, and I will bless your name."

Now the mother, you'll see, was deceitful as could be. She convinced Jacob to pretend to be

Esau, the son the only one, who receives the birthright of privileges for life.

Isaac, being old and dim in sight, never realized he gave Esau's birthright

To a conniving son and a deceitful mother; Esau lost out thus begins his plight.

The years passed on for Isaac's sons. There came a day when Jacob said, "I'll send word to my brother, of hopes he has recovered, from the error of my ways, I regret those days."

But a messenger came and this he said, "Esau, your brother is on his way.

"He's not alone, four hundred men will come to meet with you, and this is true."

Jacob was afraid of what was said, sending his family away only he stayed.

And then came a man, an angel of God, who wrestled with Jacob till night was dawn.

But Jacob was determined to do whatever it takes to receive his blessings before the break of day.

Stage Exit

If there is a dream in your heart, you should follow it and not give up. I heard Pastor Joel Osteen say, "The biggest treasures on earth are not found in the diamond mines of Africa but in the graveyards." Because there lie many dreams of those who had ambitions of becoming writers, singers, teachers, and so many other dreams that die with the dream holder.

Sometimes we do whatever it takes to get what we want. We must remember that all gain should be done in all honesty.

Backdrop 38

I became fascinated with the life of an eagle after listening to "No More Sheets" ministered by Prophetess Juanita Bynum. It amazed me how an eagle keeps the same mate for life and even more amazing was how a female eagle chooses her mate.

Rhythm 38

Can You Catch Me?

Dedicated to husbands and wives:

When times are hard and things look bad, are you by my side as the Lord said, "Do not fear, do not be dismayed, I'm here with you until the end of days"?

I'm flying high, soaring through the sky. Can I trust and believe you are by my side? My spirit is weak, my confidence is bleak, I'm about to crash. Can you catch me fast?

I'm soaring a little higher because this is my desire, to be clear and free of trouble around me, but I'm falling quickly, faster and faster. I'm going down. Can you catch me in time before I hit the ground?

I'm feeling great! I must say I'm flying so high, it takes my breath away. Now here comes trouble, bigger than before, and once again, I'm falling even more from a higher attitude, a higher altitude. Can I trust and rely you are by my side?

I'm falling so fast, and when I look over to see by my side is not where you should be; I need you beneath me. I'm about to crash. I'm about to fall. I need you to catch me before I lose it all.

Stage Exit

We exit this stage leaving a few facts about my beloved eagle. For those who have never studied the life of an eagle, it's amazing. A female eagle first tests the male to see if he is a suitable mate and can catch trouble. She takes a twig the size of an eagle's egg, flies off into the sky, drops it, and the intended mate must catch the twig before it hits the ground. Then she takes a twig the size of a baby eaglet, flies a little higher, drops it, and the intended mate must catch the twig before it hits the ground. Again, she takes a twig. This time the size of her own body weight, flies even higher, drops it, and the intended mate must catch it before it hits the ground. If the intended mate pass all the female's test, then he becomes her mate for life.

We need to know that in a relationship, we have each other's best interest at heart and will be there to support each other in the good and in the bad. We will disagree at times but should always be there to support each other. Your spouse should be your best friend, not anyone else. Spouses should be able to tell each other anything and know, "I can trust you with what I've said or with what I feel."

An eagle flies higher than any other winged creature created. Isaiah 40:31 says, "But they who wait for the Lord shall renew their strength; they shall mount up with wings like eagles; they shall run and not be weary; they shall walk and not faint." An eagle can fly high above storms. How many of us have storms in our lives that we must learn to do like the eagle and fly high above it?

An eagle can spot its prey two miles away. My takeaway: be on guard, be attentive, be as 1 Peter 5:8 says, "Be sober, be vigilant because your adversary, the devil, walks about like a roaring lion, seeking whom he may devour." Use your eagle eye and spot him miles away.

An eagle will not eat anything dead, only the living. How long do we hold on to dead things in our lives? Let it go and feed on the true and living Word of God.

An eagle makes its home in one place and one place only. Its nest can weigh up to two tons, yes tons, because an eagle continuously adds to its nest. My takeaway: stability. We all need stability in our lives. With stability we are not as one spoken of in Ephesians 4:14: "Then we will no longer be immature like children. We won't be tossed and blown about by every wind of new teaching. We will not be influenced when people try to trick us with lies so clever, they sound like the truth."

Crushing of the Spirit

In a Sunday school class one morning, God convicted me concerning guarding the heart. A church member told of an incident that resulted in hurt, shock, and disappointment. My flesh became deaf, and I was only able to hear with my spirit. I apologized with all my heart and soul, but there was still a conviction present.

I sing on my church's praise and worship team, and as I looked out into the congregation, I heard God say, "The spirit of that person has been crushed." As I thought about something crushing, I could see all the pain that can come with something being crushed. But God showed me, all crushing is not bad. What the devil meant for harm, God will turn around for good.

Olive oil was used for many things: light for lamps, healing wounds, anointing, and much more. So although the incident was one that hurt, disappointed, and shocked, I saw it as an overflow of anointing oil, not only to heal the one that was hurt, but to also encourage crushed spirits.

Backdrop 39

John 3:1–21 gives an account of a Pharisees named Nicodemus, a ruler of the Jews who had a meeting with Jesus one night. A Pharisees was a member of an ancient Jewish sect and sometimes considered self-righteous and hypocritical. Members of this group were constantly trying to find fault in Jesus, so I find it very interesting that a member of this group asked to meet with Jesus. The events leading up to Nicodemus coming to speak privately with Jesus began when he became angry because people were in the temple selling and trading. John 2:13–23 tells how Jesus overturned tables and scattered all that was in the temple. Shortly after that, Jesus was in Jerusalem at the Passover, and He did many signs and wonders. If I can use my sanctified imagination here, I would say, Nicodemus was one of the ones at the Passover witnessing the signs and wonders Jesus performed that day. I can imagine him wanting to go up to Jesus then but afraid because of the other Pharisees in the area watching him.

The following is a poem concerning the encounter of Jesus and Nicodemus. All written isn't found in the Bible; it's a way of me using my imagination about Nicodemus's thoughts and Jesus's reply.

Rhythm 39

He Came by Night

Jesus is the way, the truth, and the life; this, Nicodemus learned when he came by night. He was a ruler and a leader, prominent among men, before Jesus, Nicodemus stands. You are of God. This must be true because no other person can do what you do. So how can it be that you do all which I see; is there a secret withheld from me?

Jesus spoke and to Nicodemus he said, "My Father in heaven is the only way. You must be committed and born again. You must be willing to turn away from sin.

"But I am old, as you can see, a babe again I could never be. My mother carried me in her womb, and at an appointed time, I was born. So I came through her. The process of birth, the words you speak have me perplexed. How can I, being a man, enter the womb and be born again?

"All that I tell you is spiritual, you see. The process of rebirth comes through me. Not through your mother, nor through your earthly father, but through the Father in heaven who has all power. You are a ruler, a teacher among men. Why are you not able to comprehend? I am the way, the truth, and the life. I give movement to the lame and sight to the blind. I heal all diseases and raise the dead. I'm the light on a path to those that have lost the way. My God so love you that this He gave His only begotten Son to redeem and to save."

Stage Exit

Jesus welcomes everyone. No matter what the background is, He welcomes all. Even those against Him are welcome to come. The songwriter said, "Just as I am." But you will not leave the same if you are willing, once again, to allow interruptions and be changed.

Backdrop 40

"And she could by no means straight herself up" (Luke 13:11). The Bible tells of a woman who, for eighteen years, walked bent over. Can you imagine walking bent over for eighteen years? Not being able to look people directly in their eyes, always looking toward the ground more so than looking up? This woman's condition was said to be a "spirit of infirmity."

We all know there are two types of spirits: the spirit of God and the spirit of evil. The spirit of infirmity was an evil spirit placed on this woman. We have no background of her, and Luke was the only one to give an account of this woman. What we do know is an evil spirit was on her and the reason for her walking bent over. Unlike the woman with the issue of blood, who sought help for twelve years, the Bible gives no background of this woman seeking help for her infirmity. It's possible because it was from an evil spirit, she felt there was no need to seek help. On the other hand, maybe she sought help. At any rate, we know that something happened in her life to cause (as Jesus stated "whom Satan has bound," NKJV) this infirmity. No matter what binds us in life, one touch of Jesus will heal.

Martin Luther King Jr., said, "A man can't ride your back unless it is bent." All we need to do is put ourselves in the presence of Jesus, and He is certain to straighten up our lives.

Rhythm 40

Straighten Up!

While teaching in the synagogue on a beautiful Sabbath day, a woman with an infirmity came to hear what Jesus had to say. She had been bent over for a period of eighteen years, I'm sure she shed many tears.

She said not a word; her infirmity was heard. When Jesus saw her bound, his words were profound: "Woman, you are loosed from your infirmity."

He laid his hands on her, and immediately she was free.

She straightened up herself and glorified the Lord. If we could go back in time, we would see tears fall.

And then there was one, a ruler among the Son, who spoke up to say, "This is the Sabbath day."

There are six days in the week of which people should be healed, but on the Sabbath day, the sick should stay away.

But Jesus, knowing his heart, set him apart from all that was good, chastised him where he stood.

"So are you to say, that on this day, your animals would go uncared for because you are so careful to uphold this Sabbath day, of what you believe should be the way. No one working good deeds, this is the Old Testament's way?

"But I am the One as you have seen who raised the dead, cured all manner of diseases."

"We are no longer under the Law. I healed my daughter, this you saw."

"So you may go your merry way. I AM is a healer, every day."

And after saying these things, all His adversaries were put to shame, the people rejoiced; He restored what was lost.

Stage Exit

Life can be overwhelming at times. And it may seem as though we have the weight of the world on our shoulder. It could make us feel bent over spiritually. God is a healer of all manner of disease. Let's break it down: dis-ease. Basically, we are not at ease. God can cleanse all that ails us.

Guard the Heart

Many years ago, I worked with a lady other people on the job tried to avoid. This lady was a single mom, and from her conversations, the child's father wasn't in their lives.

Every morning (and I mean faithfully) when someone would say, "Good morning," her reply was just "Morning." I can't ever remember a day when she would say, "Good morning." As I worked with her and listened to her conversation, I began to hear a lot of pain in her life. Unfortunately, I didn't try to give her any words of encouragement.

One day, we had a staff meeting, and each person there was given the opportunity to voice her opinion. As I listened to what others had to say, I heard God say, "Guard people's heart." I shared that phrase with the others.

What God was saying is this: people don't always know what other people are going through. Sometimes people have ugly attitudes and not a pleasure to be around. Chances are, those are the people that need the people of God the most.

We should always learn to guard people's heart. You don't need to know all the details of a person's life to guard their heart; pray for them and with them. Give that friendly smile and a word of encouragement no matter how unpleasant he or she may be. Think of it as your own heart, and guard another's heart as your own. Caution: make sure your heart is after God's heart.

Backdrop 41

Several years ago, the wife of the late Bishop Phillip Davis, Cynthia Davis, took a trip to Africa while Bishop Davis remained in the states. I remember during the Sunday morning service Bishop Davis saying he had received a call from his wife that wanted to let him know "I am living in your tomorrow, and I want you to know tomorrow is going to be all right." This was said because of the time difference which made it Monday morning in Africa. I will forever remember those words because they were so profound. There is an old Gospel song that says, "One day at a time, sweet Jesus, that's all I'm asking of you."

It amazed me that there was a part of the world that was already living in the next day.

Rhythm 41

Living in Your Tomorrow

If I delight myself in the way of the Lord, the desires of my heart, He will not withhold.

I must trust, and I must believe, that the promises of God will far exceed. Everything I hope for and everything I need will be granted to me when I follow His lead.

One day at a time, this day is mine to do my best, not fail the test.

I do not know what tomorrow brings; will it bring sunshine or will it bring rain?

But this I know and can be rest assured, God is living in my tomorrow.

Step-by-step can be hard at times; I must keep my mind on God all the time.

Yesterday is gone; it never stays. I must live my life only in today. Each new day that comes my way, new mercies are given for that day.

God is living in my tomorrow. For this very reason, I hold no sorrows because He loves me so much. I feel His touch as I make my way through all my days.

Stage Exit

We exit this stage with confidence that God holds our future. His plan is for it to be full of hope and prosperity.

Backdrop 42

In the United States, car manufactures are required to print on the side-view mirror of the passenger side, "Objects in mirror are closer than they appear." This is a safety measure to help the driver avoid an accident. While listening to a Sunday morning sermon by my pastor, Vincent Riley, and thinking about the warning printed on the side-view mirror, it reminded me of God's promises. You may ask, "How does a car's side-view mirror reminds anyone of God's promise?" Well, by now, you should know the answer is found in the rhythm.

Rhythm 42

Objects May Appear

God's promises are never-ending.

He said if from the very beginning.

He created man in His image and gave him authority to conquer the enemy.

He promised to be with us always, even until the end of days. And to ensure the end will not come, He promised us His only begotten Son.

He promised to never leave nor forsake us; a reservation in heaven is what He gave us.

If we trust and obey, God's Word is the only way.

Sometimes things may get rough and God's promises may seem far from us; look at it as in the side-view mirror, and you will see His promises much nearer.

Make God the desire of your heart so the Bible's promises will never depart from the vision you have in sight; it is your rebirth right.

Stage Exit

And with this Stage Exit, we remember the saints of old: "He may not come when you want him, but He'll be there right on time."

If we look at God's promises through the naked eye, they seem so far away. But if we use a "side view mirror" mentality, they are closer than they appear.

GPS from Bitter to Better

The book of Ruth begins by telling of tragic loss but ends in undying love. Naomi lost her husband and her two sons. Only she and her daughters-in-law were left. Naomi urged the women to return to their own people because she had nothing else to give. One daughter-in-law, Orpah, listened to Naomi and went back home. Ruth, on the other hand, didn't. Ruth told Naomi, "You are my family and where you go, I'll go, your God is now my God, where you die is where I will die."

The loss of her husband and sons changed Naomi's outlook on life. She advised people to no longer call her Naomi but Mara, meaning, bitter. Thinking back to "The Unexpected," unfair things happen in life, and we don't always understand why. But remember: we will understand it better by and by. It doesn't say, "We will understand it bitter by and by."

The reality is we hurt, and we won't always understand why certain things happen that brings hurt to our lives. God understands. "He heals the brokenhearted and binds up their wounds" (Psalm 147:3).

Overcoming hurt is not easy, and it takes time. Sometimes it takes new beginnings as with Ruth and Naomi. Sometimes it takes something someone said, as in my case. Remember, it's so important to tell your story because God also heals through people. Don't ever allow the enemy to bind you in guilt and shame. You never know, your downfall may be the next person's uplifting.

I was on my way to a life of bitterness. I allow anger to linger inside of me too long. One way to avoid becoming bitter is to keep the Word of God in your life. This comes in many forms: reading God's Word, church, family, loyal friends, television/radio ministry, and inspirational music.

You also must be willing to surround yourself with people that will hold you accountable for what you are doing that is not Christlike. Stop telling your woes to the ones who are willing to bring refreshments to your pity party. Tell your story to the one you know is a pity party crasher.

This is the one that will allow you to get it all out, allow you to cry on their shoulder, the one that will say, "I love you very much, but_____."

When I was a little girl, my grandmother would make me and my cousins take castor oil. That was the most awful thing in the entire world to take. And she wouldn't make us take a small teaspoon of it; we had to take a big tablespoon dose. Her reason: "It's gonna clean out your system." And back then, the understood command was "You better not run, you better not hide, you better not spit it out, all you better do is open your month wide and swallow!"

As nasty as castor oil maybe, it's good for the insides. It cleans out the junky stuff in our bodies. We need to keep godly people in our lives that don't mind giving us a big dose of castor oil every now and then to clean out the junky stuff.

I don't know who this message will help but God Provides Strength (GPS) as we travel through this thing called life. The distance from bitter to better depends solely on us precisely following our GPS.

GPS from Worry to Worship

One Sunday morning, my pastor delivered a sermon that encouraged me to add to my GPS passage. One phrase was moving from worry to worship.

"If you pray, don't worry. If you worry, don't pray." I hear this all the time, but do I really adhere to it? I would say not because I find myself worrying about things. I don't know where this quote comes from, but it's one we must keep in front of us always. The Bible tells us in Psalms 121:4 (NKJV): "Behold, He who keeps Israel Shall neither slumber nor sleep."

We quite often say, "Easier said than done." Well, it really boils down to: are we truly putting our trust in God?

GPS from Problem to Praise

Now chances are, you will not find a breakdown of the word *problem*. So allow me to give my thoughts to encouraging the soul.

The prefix of problem is "pro." A pro is someone great at whatever is being done (pro-football or pro-basketball). "Blem" is part of the word blemish (you will not find "blem" in the dictionary). A blemish is said to be a small imperfection or a mark that spoils the appearance of something. In the Bible, when the Israelites were about to exit Egypt, God instructed them to put on their door post, the blood of a lamb that was without spot or blemish. Exodus 12:5 says, "Your lamb shall be an unblemished male a year old, you may take it from the sheep or from the goats."

So when we go around confessing to have problems, in essence, we are saying, "I am a pro at having blemishes." Let's change what we are speaking (Proverbs 18:21 [NLT]: "The tongue can bring death or life; those who love to talk will reap the consequences.") I'm in no way saying to ignore our cares. What I am saying is don't make a care a problem. God cares about everything we are concerned about. He said to cast all our cares on Him because He cares for us. What we must learn to do is exactly what Pastor Riley said and turn your "problem into praise."

When we praise God, we thank Him despite the problem. The more we praise, the smaller the problem gets until it is no longer visible. We thank Him in advance for how He will turn things around. And even if it doesn't work out the way we planned, we still praise Him.

I learned a valuable lesson from my son, William, who at the time was ten years old. He was preparing for the End of Grade (EOG) testing. I advised him to take his time completing the test, to use every second available, and to, above all, pray. I'm proud to say that he passed the test. But what encouraged me was what he said he prayed. He said he prayed to God to help him pass the test, and even if he didn't pass, everything was going to be all right. As an adult, I wouldn't have had a mind-set as his.

It's not easy doing as Paul said: being content in whatever situation we are in (Philippians 4:11). Once you get into praise mode for what was done to you in the past, it will spill over into the present.

You will find yourself with such an abundance until you will have no other choice but praise Him for what is to come. So praise Him in advance. Thus, with GPS, you will travel from problem to praise.

Backdrop 43

1 Kings 18

Elijah was a mighty prophet of God, and in his lifetime, he saw God do amazing things. It was Elijah who killed the prophets of Baal by calling down fire from heaven. It was Elijah who spoke the Word of God to a widow urging her to feed him before she fed herself and her son with what little flour and oil she had left. The Word of God spoken to the widow along with her obedience caused her bin of flour and her jar of oil to never go dry. It was that same Elijah who, when the widow's son became ill and he died, restored life to the child. Indeed, I would say, Elijah saw God do some amazing things. But what happens when you see the hand of God doing mighty works in your life then allow something someone said or did bring fear to your life?

Rhythm 43

Why Are You Running?

Elijah was a prophet of God, and for this reason, Elijah was called to bring law and order back to the land and put Baal to shame. So he spoke to and challenged the people, "How long will you waver between two opinions? If you believe in God, serve Him, but if Baal is god, follow him!" In other words, what Elijah said was "Make up your mind at this time. This back-and-forth thing you do, you can't serve the Lord and Baal too." So the prophets of Baal were called *450 in all.*

Elijah, the prophet of God, faced Baal's prophets, *no fear at all.* He told them to build an altar, prepare a bull for an offering. Elijah did the same and instructed they call on the name of their god whom they serve to send down fire from above. And the one who answers the call is the living god of us all. The prophets did as Elijah said, prepared the bull, and said, "O Baal, answer us," calling from morning until dust. They called and called Baal's name, but everything remained the same; no fire came from above. Baal didn't answer the call.

God's former altar was torn down, and Elijah said, "My turn now." He began to rebuild God's altar, the beginning of law and order. He dug a trench in the ground, twelve stones he found, placed them around the altar, then gave this order: "Fill the trench with water, three times over was the order." Elijah did the same and then called on the name of the one and true living God, then fire begin to fall, consuming the altar and all. The true God answered the call; even the water was consumed; the prophets of Baal now doomed. And the people fell to their face, much shame and disgrace; and they called on the name of the Lord, declaring He is God, once and for all!

The prophets of Baal were seized. God commanded Elijah to lead the prophets down to a brook, and it was there Elijah took each life of Baal's prophets that were in sight. The prophets of Baal were no more; this made their leader sore.

The leader and biggest sinner of all, Jezebel is what she was called. She's behind all this mess; she was Elijah's great test. When Jezebel heard her prophets were dead, a message to Elijah in essence said, "Pray your God reach me first. If not, I'll bury you in the dust. You will be dead by this time tomorrow. You killed my prophets. I'll make you sorry."

All that was seen and all the Lord had done, vanished from Elijah's thinking; his faith started sinking. He ran for his life out of Jezebel's sight. He was afraid of what she said; he hid for many days. As he sat under a juniper tree, he basically said, "O Lord, kill me!" He fell asleep under that tree; the angel of God woke him from his sleep and at that time commanded he eat. The journey ahead was much to bear. He met with God and this God shared, "Go stand on the mountain. I will pass by you there and give you a word for what you must do to anoint those that are to follow you."

A great wind came; the Lord was not there. An earthquake came; He was not there. Then came fire; the Lord was not there. A gentle whisper came, in essences, God proclaimed, "Go back the way from which you came. Jezebel, the enemy, no longer threatens your name.

"I will take care of her and her evil deeds. Dogs will devour her and all who followed her lead. Continue your mission, this I say: bring back law and order to the land this day."

Stage Exit

This stage brings to light that even the great prophets of God faced fear. But God has a word for fear. First John 4:18: "Perfect love [God's love] cast out all fear."

Backdrop 44

Second Kings 4 tells the story of a woman that had no children. By reading the passage, it leads us to believe that she and her husband (or maybe just her husband) are beyond childbearing years. This lady is referred to in the Bible as "The Shunammite Woman." She perceived Elisha to be a man of God and encouraged her husband to build a special room for him since he frequently came to their city. Elisha was extremely grateful and asked what he could do to return the favor. The Shunammite replied she needed no favors since she had everything she needed. But Elisha insisted something be granted to her. Elisha's servant noticed the couple had no children and advised Elisha of this. During those days, if a woman didn't have any children, chances are, it wasn't by choice but the inability to conceive. Elisha told the Shunammite that at a certain time, she would have a son, and it came to pass as Elisha promised. The child was born but became ill later in his childhood and died. Let's read how the Shunammite reacted to the death of her son.

Rhythm 44

All Is Well

You said, "All is well?" Hmm, I can't tell. My bills are due, and I haven't a clue how to pay my rent; my money spent on so many things. I throw up my hands. I'm ready to give up. I look at my cup. I see it's half empty and consequently, I have no more to give, so how do I live and keep the faith for another day?

The Bible records, and I know it's true, of a Shunammite woman and this she knew. Elisha the prophet, was a man of God; a double portion of Elijah's spirit he inherits from God. And each time he came the Shunammite's way, she opened her home and there he stayed. She said to her husband, "This we should do. Make a small room on the roof, put in a bed, a table, a chair too, and a lamp for him so when he comes through, he'll have a place he can call his own. He'll have a place just like home."

Elisha was pleased with the work that was done. In appreciation he said, "You will give birth to a son. About this time next year, you will hold him in your arms." The Shunammite was surprised; she couldn't remain calm.

At the appointed time as Elisha said, she gave birth to a son; what a glorious day. But something happened, and the boy said, "My head! My head!" and then he was dead. The Shunammite mother went and laid her lifeless son's body on Elisha's bed. A donkey was saddled; she began to ride as fast as she could to where Elisha resided. When he saw her coming a distance away, he said to his servant, "Run her way, find out what's wrong. Is it her husband or son?" The servant went and as Elisha said, he asked the Shunammite, "What's wrong this day?"

"All is well" was her reply. The Shunammite mother continued to ride. When she got to the prophet, she grabbed hold of his feet and said to Elisha, "The son you gave me, I didn't ask you for him. This was your plan. Now he's dead."

Elisha got up and followed her home, went up to his room, laid on her son. Life returned to the Shunammite's son. Now I can tell, all is well.

Stage Exit

Just in case you missed it, I will like to bring this to your attention before we exit this stage. The Shunammite woman was stopped a few times as she made her way to Elisha. Elisha's servant continued to ask what the matter was. Each time she said, "All is well." I don't know about you, but under such conditions, I wouldn't be able to say, "All is well" and my child has just died.

All though she said all is well, all was not well in her spirit. If it were, she would've told her husband the child is dead and buried him. Also, she didn't waste time telling those unable to help her. She went directly to the one she knew could restore life.

So remember this: during dead times in our lives, it's not always wise to tell your story to everyone, only to the ones you know are God sent.

Behind the Scenes

Each morning before I take my son to school, we will pray. Sometimes I would forget, and he will remind me, "We didn't pray." One morning as I was taking him to school, we had a conversation about a few bad dreams he had that night and asked had I ever had bad dreams. I told him, "Yes." I told him when I have bad dreams, I would repeat over and over, "Jesus Christ is my Lord and Savior."

I explained to William that although his body is asleep, his spirit never sleeps, and that it is possible to say what I told him to say. As I continued to try and give comfort, I began explaining about the spirit. I told William he must be careful of the things watched on TV, music he listens to, and even the games he plays on his Xbox. I let him know the reason I don't allow him to play, watch, or listen to just anything is because things can get into the spirit.

About nineteen years ago, I was a stay-at-home mom and watched soap operas faithfully. Nothing was done in my house until after the soaps were done. I watched them so much until I started dreaming about them, what will happen, and what I wanted to happen on the shows.

I was in church one Sunday morning. There was a guest speaker. Lo and behold, he started talking about how addicted people were to TV and made a special mention of soap operas. My thoughts were, "You must be kidding me. Why are you coming down my street, knocking on my door with the audacity to step on my toes. All of 'em?" At any rate, I stopped watching soap operas.

My daughter Amanda was about nine months old at the time, and we didn't have cable. I never liked talk shows, so that left ETV. All day long my TV was on ETV: *Sesame Street, Mr. Rogers Neighborhood*, and all that good stuff.

During that time, I didn't know something was going on behind the scene. Two days before Amanda's second birthday, my mom and I were out shopping for items for her birthday party. My mom had on a T-shirt from a family reunion. Amanda pointed at a letter and said what my mom thought was the word *cow*. She then said, "That's not a cow, Amanda."

I would guess, in her almost two-year-old mind, Amanda said, "I didn't say cow." Amanda then began to point to letters and numbers on my mom's T-shirt, saying what each one was. We almost pass out!

At that point, we found different things and asked Amanda what the letter or number was. She was able to say what each letter and number was; it blew my mind. I started thinking back to how in the world a child not quite two years old was able to do this. Then I remembered, over a year of watching nothing but ETV. It was at that point, I grasped what the minister had said so long ago when he preached on how the things we watch get in our spirits.

Be careful of what you watch, listen to, and the games you play; it has a tendency of becoming your desires. Be careful of your desires; they have a tendency of becoming what you pursue. Be careful of what you pursue; it has a tendency of becoming what you gain. Be careful of what you gain; it has a tendency of becoming what controls you.

Don't ever think, "Oh, it's just a TV show or just a movie or just a game. I don't see the harm." If this is your mentality, then I'm afraid the enemy has you where he wants you.

On April 20, 1999, two teenage boys opened fire on many innocent people, and many lost their lives. Behind the scene, these boys were in their rooms, no prior arrests or trouble in school nor out robbing banks or carjacking people; they were simply in their rooms playing video games.

A young man opened fire in a Colorado movie theater during the opening of *Batman: The Dark Knight Rises*. This young man worked as a camp counselor for underprivileged kids one summer.

Prior to the shooting, he dyed his hair red to resemble the character of the Joker.

We can go on and on of the many tragic killings where disturbed individuals opened fire on innocent people at schools, shopping malls, and even churches. But somewhere behind the scenes, something went terribly wrong; no one paid attention to what was going on behind the scenes.

So, what is our part in this? First Peter 5:8 says, "Be sober, be vigilant because the devil walks about like a roaring lion, seeking whom he may devour." So we take notice of every little thing no matter how insignificant it may seem.

First Thessalonians 5:17 says, "Pray without ceasing." Some people may say, "It doesn't take all of that." I beg to differ. It takes seeking the face of God always. Sometimes we must be the nosy neighbor. And remember, your neighbor isn't limited to who lives next door or across the street. Being nosy is okay when it saves lives.

Backdrop 45

During Jesus's walk on this earth, there were not many homes He was welcomed in. One of the homes He was welcomed in was Pete's (Luke 4:38–39). And I strongly believe it was at Peter's house where the four friends tore off the roof and lowered their friend down to Jesus (Luke 5:18–20). There was the home of Jairus when he healed his daughter (Mark 5:38–43). He also called up to Zacchaeus in a sycamore fig tree and told Zacchaeus he would come to his home (Luke 19:1–9). And then there was Mary and Martha (Luke 10:38–42).

Rhythm 45

At His Feet

Like a little child anxiously waiting to hear a story;
I sit at the master's feet.
Gazing up at His radiant face I sit at the master's feet.
When I sit at the master's feet, my spirit and soul begin to weep.
He understands my pain and sorrows and speaks life into my tomorrow.
When I sit at the master's feet I listen intently as He speaks.
No time for a busy day.
No time for trouble in my way.
No time to worry about what went wrong.
No time to listen to sad songs.
No time to be discouraged by what others say;
Jesus the Christ is the only way.
I'll sit at the master's feet; only He makes my life complete.

Stage Exit

As the pitter-patter of our feet exit the stage, let's be committed to sitting at the feet of Jesus. This means we are willing to not come with a list of problems but to say, "I love being in Your presence. There is no other place I would rather be." In Luke 10:38–42, Jesus and the disciples came to a village where a certain woman name

Martha and her sister Mary welcomed them into their home. Mary sat at the feet of Jesus as Martha prepared dinner for everyone. She became upset that she was doing all the work while Mary sat at Jesus's feet. But the Lord said, "My dear Martha, you are worried and upset over all these details! There is only one thing worth being concerned about. Mary has discovered it, and it will not be taken away from her."

Let's get busy doing God's business and not all other business. Luke 2:49: "Why were you looking for me? Didn't you know I must be about my Father's business?" Martha was about doing the business of others. When Jesus spoke, he spoke of the Father and the kingdom. By sitting at His feet, Mary was about doing the business of God by listening to what Jesus had to say.

Backdrop 46

Long Weekend

There are a few holidays that results in long weekends: Good Friday, Memorial Day, Labor Day, Martin Luther King Jr. Day, and Presidents' Day. These holidays are a way of honoring men and women who served this country in one way or another. And of course, Good Friday is a reminder of the ultimate sacrifice of our Lord and Savior.

Many people enjoy a long weekend during these holidays: a Friday, Saturday and Sunday, or a Saturday, Sunday and Monday. While sitting in a Wednesday night service leading up to Good Friday and Easter Sunday, the term long weekend came to mind. I started to think about the fact that so many people will enjoy a long weekend because of Good Friday. However, it was my belief that many people would partake in celebrating a long weekend without really celebrating the reason behind the long weekend.

Rhythm 46

A long weekend, most of us see, as a way of relaxing and being set free. From the hustle and bustle of the passing week, three long days are headed our way. Will we show honor where it's due, to the ones that paved the way for me and for you? A long weekend, let's make some plans to give honor where honor is due for those that sacrificed their lives for me and for you.

Stage Exit

Short, sweet, and to the point. As we celebrate these holidays, please, let's not just see it as a break from work or school or as just a long weekend. But take the time to remember the reason for the season.

Back against the Wall

How many times have you felt as if your back was against the wall and you had nowhere to turn? We all have faced a place of seemingly being defeated. Sometimes when we feel our backs are against the wall, we come out swinging. Sometimes we stand or slouch down in defeat. But I heard of a man whose back was against the wall. A sentence of death was decreed. The man I speak of was Hezekiah (2 Kings 20). When you find your back against the wall, turn around and face it, just as Hezekiah did. In other words, face what you feel is against you opposed to running for it.

At the age of twenty-five, Hezekiah became king and ruled over Judah. Second Kings 18 tells how Hezekiah put all his trust in God and obeyed the commandments given to Moses by God. But still, God gave a decree for Hezekiah to get his house in order because he was soon to die.

I would say that King Hezekiah's back was against the wall. During his reign, he was forced to pay tribute to the enemy. King Hezekiah was up against the king of Assyria, Sennacherib. King Sennacherib sent a message to King Hezekiah that basically said, "You are no match for me, King of Assyria."

Hezekiah spoke words of encouragement to Judah, assuring them there was no cause to be afraid. "Be strong and courageous. Do not be afraid or discouraged because of the king of Assyria and the vast army with him." With him is only the arm of flesh, but with us is the Lord our God to help us and to help us fight our battles.

The people of Judah gained confidence in Hezekiah's words. But King Sennacherib spoke the opposite and told the people of

Judah not to put their trust in what Hezekiah said. King Sennacherib pointed out that the Lord God of which Hezekiah believed in was not able to deliver people from his grip. He referenced all the countries in the past that depended on their god to deliver with no prevail.

In a case as this one, we must know who our God is. It was true that other false gods were not able to deliver; so again, we must recognize who our God is. He is above all that is in heaven, on earth, and beneath the earth. He is the Alpha and the Omega, the beginning and the end. He can part the waters of the sea; He delivers from the belly of a whale and the fire of a furnace. He raised the stench of death after four days and breathed life into dry bones. He commands an alarm clock to wake us up.

When Hezekiah was faced with death, he turned and faced the wall and pleaded his case. As a result, God added fifteen years to his life. When your back is against the wall, don't allow yourself to be pinned there. Turn around and face it, being certain you have strong evidence to back up your case when you begin to remind God of all the works you have done in his name.

Backdrop 47

After the resurrection of Jesus, He appeared to the disciples, Mary, and many others. Peter had decided to go fishing, and the other disciples decided to go with Him. After a night of fishing, they caught nothing. When morning came, Jesus stood on the shore and called to them to cast their nets on the right side of the boat. Peter was reluctant at first but listened to the voice far away. They cast a net on the right side of the boat and caught so many fish until the net almost broke. Then John realized the person who stood on the shore was Jesus. Immediately Peter jumped into the water and started swimming toward Jesus (John 21:1–7). This is the same Peter who, when Jesus bid him to walk on the water toward him, he did. The other disciples returned to shore in the boat. Once they were all together again, they enjoyed a fish breakfast by the sea; how awesome that must've been.

Rhythm 47

I Will Do Anything!

I will do anything just to get to you; walk on water if you told me to.

I will do anything just to get to you; jump in headfirst and swim the ocean blue.

I will do anything to get to you; cut off the ear of any trying to harm you.

I will do anything to get to you; just to behold the glory of you.

I will do anything to get to you; forsake this world; its riches too.

I will do anything to spread your name; stand before men; no condemnation; no shame.

I will do anything to praise your name; die to self, it is You who reigns.

Stage Exit

Remember when many turned away from Jesus because they didn't fully understand what was said? Remember: Peter said, "Lord, to who shall we go? You have eternal life" (John 6:68).

Another of Jesus's disciples said, "Let us also go, that we may die with him" (John 11:16).

Then there was Zacchaeus: "Behold Lord, the half of my goods I give to the poor; and if I have taken anything from any man by false accusations, I restore him fourfold" (Luke19:8).

And let's not forget Mary. She poured expensive oil on the feet of Jesus, washed them with her tears and dried his feet with her hair; kissing them continuously (John 12:3). All are accounts of, "I'll do anything" for the sake of Jesus Christ.

Backdrop 48

Judges 13–16 tells the story of Sampson's birth and life. An angel of God visited Sampson's mother and gave her instruction of what she was to do during her pregnancy and how she should raise her son. God instructed that Sampson was to never cut his hair, among other things. During this time, the Israelites did evil things in the sight of the Lord. As a result, God handed the Israelites over to the Philistines. If you remember, the Philistines were the people David defeated by bringing down Goliath. God gave Sampson strength beyond what was normal for a human. Sampson's mission was to deliver the Israelites out of the hands of the Philistines. When the Philistines saw how strong Sampson was, they wondered how one man could be so strong. They hired a woman named Delilah to find out where his strength lies.

I remember a sermon by the late Bishop Davis concerning Sampson. He stated Sampson must not have been a big muscular man (as pictures depict) because if he was, then no one would have questioned where his strength lies. But that Sampson must have been a small slender man which caused someone to think how a person of this size could be so strong.

Rhythms 48

A Spirit of Delilah

Why do we sometimes choose to play with fire?

The name of the game is called Delilah.

It's not a he nor a she; it's a spirit of enticement so we must flee.

Why do I need to know this you say?

"I can't be enticed by this spirit," you may say.

Beware of Delilah, this spirit is strong.

It doesn't take no for an answer, it continues on.

Poking and begging until you give in; this spirit doesn't quit until you submit:

Your time, your gifts, your money, and your life; be strong in the Lord, both day and night.

Delilah is a spirit that can lead to destruction anytime we choose not to follow God's instructions.

Listen to this, it's filled with tricks.

How Sampson fell prey to Delilah's display.

Sampson decided to play with fire; the name of the game still called Delilah.

Sampson clearly knew he wasn't to cut his hair, for therein lied his strength, his anointing was there.

And Sampson clearly knew the game Delilah played but he was so enticed by the love it gave.

And Sampson clearly heard Delilah's request: "Tell me what makes you strong, so you can be overcome."

That was clear enough to see, anyone should have enough sense to flee.

But Sampson did the same, and he played the Delilah game;

"Tie me with seven fresh bowstrings that have not been dried, this is where my strength lie."

Delilah did exactly as Sampson said; she tied him with seven fresh bowstrings; that wasn't where Sampson's strength could be found.

Delilah was upset that Sampson lied.

Once again Sampson played the Delilah game: "Tie me with new ropes that have never been used. After that I won't be able to move."

Delilah did exactly as Sampson said: she tied him up with ropes that were new, and when the enemy came, he broke those too.

The spirit of Delilah is furious by now; like a little child in a candy store, it threw a tantrum on the ground.

"All this time you've made a fool of me. Where lies your strength? Please tell me how to tie you up, how you may be subdued. Tell me now, I look like a fool."

Once again Sampson played the Delilah game: "Seven braids are on my head. Tie them and tighten them on a loom. I will become weak as any man. I will be doomed."

So Delilah did exactly as Sampson said: tied his braids and then she said, "Sampson, the Philistines are upon you!"

But Sampson broke free, made the Philistines flee.

Delilah then questioned, "How can you say you love me?"

The game is now over; Sampson gave in. "Cut the locks of my hair. I'll become as weak as any man."

Delilah did exactly as Sampson said; when the Philistines came, he could not get away.

His strength had left him; his gift was gone; when you play with fire, you tend to get burned.

Spirits are real and this we must know.

The enemy roams to and fro.

Seeking whom he may devour, life is not a game; follow God's instructions and you will gain blessings from God, again and again.

Stage Exit

We must be careful of what we allow in our spirit. Years ago, Bishop T.D. Jakes preached a sermon titled "Brother, that's Entrapment." He gave an illustration of a moth being drawn to the light. As a moth gets closer to the light, it's obvious: the light is hot, but the moth is drawn to the light although it means danger. The point that was made is we see the danger ahead, but we continue to pursue it. Let's commit to living our lives, not playing with fire.

Permanent Decision, Temporary Situation

While speaking to an associate one day, this person stated how terrible things were going in their life and those things brought on suicidal thoughts. I'm not a psychiatrist, counselor, or doctor by any means, but my response was the title of my message: "That's a permanent decision for a temporary situation."

So many people live in pain: physical, emotional, and mental. Suicide is sweeping the nation, and it's sad to hear that someone took their own life because they felt this was the only way to stop the pain. Pain that lingers leads to dark places. Don't allow yourself to remain in dark places. Muster up as much strength as you possibly can to pull yourself out of those dark places. And if you can't do that, be mindful of the people in your life because someone can help.

Don't be ashamed to express your true feelings concerning the depts of pain. Be open and transparent; let someone you trust know how you feel. By doing this, you have a trusted confidant who will check on you and make him/herself available for you. Don't allow the enemy to overpower your mind. His goal is to kill. He will whisper in your ear, "No one cares about you. Why are you even here?" His goal is to steal. He will try to steal your joy, your peace and respect for your own life. And his goal is to destroy. He will destroy your life and the lives of others who love you.

Life is worth living. Things may get hard, but life is worth living. Never allow anyone define who you are. Never allow anything nor anyone have power over you. Our Father in heaven and His spirit that lives in us should be all that powers over us. Those that are called by His name are His awesome creations, and that's what matters.

There are some decisions we make, and there's no turning back. Please seek help in situations you face that seem beyond bearable.

Backdrop 49

So much trouble came Job's way until he said it would have been better if he had never been born (Job 3:1–3, NLT). So much trouble came Elijah's way that he asks God to kill him (1 Kings 19:3–4, NLT). And King David had so much trouble on his track that he wrote many psalms, crying out to God. Trouble is sure to come our way. But God!

Rhythm 49

Trouble in My Way

Today was difficult for me; I fell and that hurt me, you see.

I came to the end of my rope. I'm on the ground; I have no more hope.

I have reasoned, I have screamed, and I have yelled.

I know, the latter two will never compel; a change to come my way; my patience is gone, I must say.

I did all that I knew to do. Then God said, "Are you through trying to do what only I can do?"

I'm discouraged, I'm hurt, and I'm lost. I have counted the cost of all the trouble I have gone through. In the end, God, there's only you.

Only you can take away my pain. Only you can bring my searching to an end.

Only you can fill the empty space by replacing it with your mercy and grace.

Stage Exit

We exit this stage with this quote: "Let go and let God."

Backdrop 50

First Samuel 24:1–13 is the story of how David had the opportunity to kill King Saul but didn't because of his relationship with God and I would say, his conscience. Saul had tried relentlessly to kill David, and this was information that David was very aware of. There is an old saying that goes "Let your conscience be your guide." Things don't always go as we planned. Some are big disappoints, and some makes you "flat-out angry." It's up to us how we handle disappointments and how we deal with the anger.

The Bible says, "Be ye angry, and sin not: let not the sun go down upon your wrath" (Ephesians 4:26–27, KJV). I thank God for His never-ending grace and mercy; I have allowed the sun to go down on my wrath many, many nights. Just know that anger is not where the sin lie but how we handle the anger could lead to sin.

Rhythm 50

My God Won't Allow Me

There was a time when I once said, "My todays are harder than my yesterdays." Things didn't go my way; I had so much I wanted to say, but the Word of God is inside of me; hence, my God won't allow me.

I want to speak my mind, but such words would be unkind to the one on the receiving end. Once it's out, I can't defend the harsh words which I just spoke; can't write it off as a joke. Can't let my anger get the best of me because the living Word is inside of me; hence, my God won't allow me.

Disappointments come my way. I long for a better day, when the pain I feel is no more because I'm very close to walking out the door, but commitment is all I see; hence, my God won't allow me.

So I walk, and I pace the floor, looking intently at the door. I have rehearsed everything I will say; a little still voice whispers, "Pray." The words I have in my mouth are not pleasant, so I stop and think before I speak because I know, my God won't allow me.

Stage Exit

We exit on this note: "If you can't say something good, then don't say anything at all." I don't always follow this rule, but I recognize this and am willing to call out for help. Help!

We Trust, We Wait, We Serve

Trust, when broken, can be difficult to fix and in some cases, doesn't get fixed. In a relationship when trust is broken, the one whose trust was betrayed may always find him/herself suspicious of the other person's actions. At 2:30 a.m., August 2010, I found myself worried and frustrated, asking God can I trust this certain person. God spoke to me as clear as a person standing with me: "All you have to do is trust Me."

I have learned that trusting God doesn't always mean to trust Him to give us what we are asking for, but to trust that He knows what is best for us. Sometimes what we ask for is not necessarily what God wants for us. And in some cases, what we are asking for is not a bad thing but may not be what God has in His plan for us. This could lead to some level of difficulty because of course, "we want what we want when we want it." So what do we do? This is a question I have struggled with for years. Here is what we do:

We trust God knowing that He has seen every tear shed and that He feels the pain of our broken hearts. It's so important for us to realize that God is not so far away from us, that He is untouchable and doesn't feel our pain. "For we do not have a High Priest who is unable to empathized with our weaknesses, but we have one who has been temped in every way, just as we are, yet he didn't sin" (Hebrew 4:15, NIV). So we trust God knowing that He cares for us and that He is the giver of life.

We wait. Waiting is hard for most of us because in our opinion, God is not working fast enough. We then take matters into our own hands, hoping to speed up the process. When the children of

Israel tried taking matters into their own hands, a few days journey turned into forty years. I can relate to this. Let the truth be told. I take matters into my own hands often. It's like trying to put a puzzle together with missing pieces or baking a cake with missing ingredients; it won't work. Therefore, we wait; only God can fill in the missing pieces and give the missing ingredients, and nothing will happen until He is ready to go forth.

I can remember one day, Pastor Melody explaining waiting on God in a way I hadn't thought of. She said it's like a waiter/waitress in a restaurant; they wait on the customer. They cater to your hungry need while you are there. We should be hungry for God and remain in His presence. They bring you what you ask for but only those things on the menu. If it's not on God's menu, don't ask for it because it's not His plan for you. And they keep coming back asking, "Is there anything else I may get for you?" We wait on God by serving other people and by doing His will. We shouldn't sit around twiddling our thumbs, waiting on God to give us what we want. We should be running to Him asking, "What else would you like for me to do, Father?"

We serve. Serving is an act of kindness to others. Putting our gifts and talents to actions to help others. We should serve others without expecting anything in return. We trust, we wait, and while we are trusting and waiting, we are also serving to bring glory to God.

Backdrop 51

In the Bible, God made promises that, because of the present circumstances, the ones He made the promise to found it hard to believe it would come to pass. There were also people whom God gave strict instruction for what should be and what shouldn't be done. But because of the flesh, disobedience came first.

Rhythm 51

This Looks So Much Like

Doubt. God made a promise to Abraham that he would have a son, but Abraham was well up in age and his childbearing days were done. Sarah, his wife, heard the promise, and this she knew was true. "I'm an old woman. Can't you see? Why do you try to fool me?" Sarah laughed within herself; she believed not what was said; she couldn't see how this could be. *This looks so much like Me.*

Complaining. Moses delivered the Israelites from the grips of an evil leader. As they journeyed to the Promised Land, Moses was an interceder. The Israelites began to complain of the journey at hand; they forgot so quickly the Red Sea; they forgot how God set them free. *This looks so much like Me.*

Disobedience. God gave Jonah an assignment, somewhat of a refinement. The people of Nineveh were wicked, so Jonah brought a ticket to flee from the message of God, to preach repentance to those involved of constant ungodly behavior. The city needed a savior. Jonah disobeyed God's command; therefore he ran, and he took a trip by sea. *This looks so much like Me.*

Forgiveness. David was a man after God's own heart. And from God, David decided he would never part. Temptation came his way. However, David didn't stray from the things that brought sin. David fast and prayed to no end. I would imagine he stayed on his knees. Oh my God, *this looks so much like Me.*

Stage Exit

I confess I am not where I should be, but I thank God I am far from what I used to be. The beginning of recovery is recognizing the need for improvement then having an action plan.

Backdrop 52

Emotional pain is difficult to deal with. Unlike physical pain, there is no over-the-counter medication you can buy to heal emotional pain. There are medications that are prescribed for depression, but do they really get to the root of the problem? Again, do not hear what I am not saying. I am not downplaying prescription medication to offset depression. Emotional pain can hurt more than any physical pain we will ever feel. Sometimes we live in denial—denial of feeling pain and denial of inflicting pain. At any rate, it hurts. Sometimes we fail to seek the only Physician that can take away the pain. Just know, God is real. Psalm 46:1 says, "God is our refuge and strength, a very present help in trouble."

Rhythm 52

It Really Happened

My hurt and pain is so real. Even though you can't feel all that I go through, I want so much to blame you. God said He's my strong tower. I can run into Him; He will give me power to endure the heartache I feel. Only God can heal.

This I know is true. I often comfort you concerning the way I feel. You in essence say it's not real and refuse to admit what's true; you would feel the same if it happened to you.

The cause of my pain is real. Those actions, I didn't imagine. I'm hurting; it really happened.

The Word of God says forgive. I have, but again and again, things remain the same. It's by a miracle I didn't go insane.

There are three sides to this story; only God's side deserves the glory. God has all the power. He heals us in His strong tower.

Stage Exit

We bring to the stage: transparency. It is so important to be open about our feelings (to those we trust). It helps with the process of healing.

Focus beyond Expectations

I like football but still have a lot to learn about the game. My favorite team is the Carolina Panthers. One of the better games played by the Panthers was against the New York Giants on October 7, 2018. During this game, quarterback Eli Manning threw a completed pass to Odell Beckham Jr. (OBJ). While all eyes on the field were focused on tackling OBJ, he threw a fifty-seven-yard touchdown pass to Saquon Barkley, who by the way, was wide open.

Carolina's defense set an expectation that OBJ would run down the field to gain as many yards as he possibly could. Therefore, all the attention was placed on the completed pass. Instead of running with the ball after the completed pass, OBJ threw the ball to teammate, Saquon Barkley, who he spotted close to the end zone. No one on Carolina's defense focused on Saquon waiting near the end zone.

That game play brought to my attention the importance of remaining focused beyond what we expect to happen. We, at times, are set in our ways or conformed to our habits. When we do this, we leave no room for greater unexpected things. If we say, "My finances are bad, and as far as I can see, they will always be that way," we set before us a life of lack. But if we look beyond the expectations we set (how we think things will play out), we will see a field of wide-open options.

We should all set goals in life. Reaching the mark of the goal takes focus and stepping out of what we know as normal. Just because you expect something to go a certain way doesn't mean it always will. Be alert, stay focused, and look beyond what you expect.

Backdrop 53

From Genesis to Revelation, we can see where God took a little and turned it into a lot.

You may think what little you have isn't going to make a difference. Well, if we get to the point where we truly trust God and give Him what we have, it will make a world of difference.

Rhythm 53

All I Have…

Genesis chapters 39-41

I sat in jail, was wrongly accused; my master's wife tried to use my looks and my stature for personal gain. My master believed it; this is insane. Year after year, I sat in jail, no chance to give my details. As I laid there each night, all I had were my dreams at night. Then one day the others who were bound with me, remembered my gift of interpreting dreams. They told my master what I could do; I interpreted his dreams, and he released me to watch over his people and over his land. All I had was a dream at hand.

Exodus 14

All I have is a staff in my hand headed toward the Red Sea; how can it be? So many people are following my track. Pharaoh's on his way to take them back. To a life of defeat, who wants that? They murmur, they grumble, they fuss and complain, they are looking at me; I'm racking my brain. How can we cross over? I don't have a plan. All I have is this staff in my hand. But the Word of God spoke to me: "Use what you have and part the Red Sea."

1 Kings 17:8–16

Things are rough; I'm about to give up. This man says to me, "Will you feed me?" I answered him truthfully; I pray he understands; a little flour and oil is all I have. This I have done as you can see; gather a few sticks for my son and for me. I'll prepare a meal this last time, after which, my son and I will die. But Elijah spoke, said, "Take all you have, feed me first. Your supply shall last." The faithful mother did as she was told; her bin was never dry because she didn't withhold the very last of all she had.

2 Kings 7

All I have are my feet. The enemy is near us; does this mean defeat? Why do we sit here waiting to die if we go to their camp, they may keep us alive? But if we stay here, it's possible we'll die. Should we go, or should we stay? I suggest, let's be on our way. If we die, we die on the move; let's make an effort; we have nothing to lose.

But when we arrived at the enemy's camp, all we feared had disappeared. For the Lord had caused the feet of four men to sound like thousands, so we marched right in.

1 Samuel 17

All I have in my bag are five smooth stones, a slingshot in my hand. I'm facing a giant, but he can't scare me. The power of God rests on me. And with all I have on this day, giants will fall, getting out of my way.

Matthew 14:13–21, Luke 9:10–17

All I have is lunch in my bag. Two fish and five loaves of bread. I will gladly share all that I have; I can't imagine how all I have will feed a multitude; how will it last? But with God's blessings, it came to be, all I had fed a multitude and me.

Ezekiel 37

All I have are these dry bones. They lay in the valley; all life is gone. Many dry bones as far as I can see; the Word of God spoke to me. Prophesy Ezekiel to these dry bones; I know you can see that life is gone.

Do you believe the word I say? Do you believe that on this day these dry bones can live again? Speak my word, and tell the four winds to breathe a breath of life to the slain, that these dry bones may live again. I will give then sinew, muscles and skin, after which, they shall live again.

Mark 12:41–44

All I have are two small coins. My bills were due; my money is gone. All I have to my name, I give my offering and I shall gain; the windows of heaven will open for me and pour me out a blessing I won't have room to receive.

Your Word

Things aren't quite as I thought it would be. I had a vision for this life You gave me. Time after time I find myself allowing circumstances to take Your place. You gave me a word, and I know it's true. Your word was clear: trust in You.

I praise You, God, because on my track grace and mercy won't allow me to go back. And sometimes it's hard to remain focused on the many words that You have spoken. The outlook of life gets blurred at times, but this I'm determined to keep in mind. You are love, and Your message is true: "For I know the plans I have for you, plans to prosper and not to harm you, plans to give you hope and a future too."

I praise You, God, for clearing the blur because all I have is Your Word.

Stage Exit

Give God all we have because He can do more with the little we have than we ever could.

Backdrop 54

A dream I had one night ended with "until you let go of the anger, you will not go anywhere." I don't recall what happened in the dream; all I remember is what was said at the end of my dream. I woke up and wrote the following poem.

Rhythm 54

So many things are weighing me down; until I release them, I'm bound to the ground. The Bible tells us to mount up like wings of an eagle. But for me, I'm too eager to fix on my own all I see as wrong. But in essence God said, "Leave it alone. Stop trying to do what only I can do. Trust in me, I'll fix it for you."

Stage Exit

Again, "Let go and let God." I will admit, a lot of my delays are due to me trying to fix things on my own.

Heed the Warnings

The East Coast was hit with two devastating hurricanes: Florence and Michael. During these hurricanes, I tracked them from the beginning to the end. There were several warnings from several groups of people: government officials, FEMA, law enforcement, rescue operators, news reporters, and civilians. Sadly, not all heed the warnings, and unfortunately, many lives were lost as a result.

Our disobedience allows history to repeat itself. Adam and Eve didn't heed God's warning to not eat from the tree of life and death. The people didn't heed the warnings of Noah telling of a flood. Lot's wife didn't heed the warning to not look back. Pharaoh didn't heed the warning to let the Hebrews go. The Israelites didn't heed Jeremiah's warnings, and the list goes on and on.

How many times have we said or heard someone else say, "Something told me to do this, or something told me to go this way"? God speaks to our spirit and warns us against danger and bad decisions. First Corinthians 10:12 says, "Therefore let him who thinks he stands take heed lest he fall." Sometimes we think our way is the best way. "Let him who thinks he stands take heed." In other words, let him who thinks he is right listen because the moment we think our choices are right, it ends up putting us in danger, especially when we choose not to heed the warnings.

I can't express enough the importance of heeding warnings. At what point will we realize it's not okay to do what we want to do when it means placing others, or ourselves, in danger? Some warnings are to save us from imminent danger, as in hurricanes. Some warnings are to save us from eternal danger, such as when God instructed

Adam and Eve not to eat from the tree of the knowledge of good and evil. The Bible gives us many warnings. The scripture that sticks with me at present is 2 Timothy 3. The Bible was written thousands of years ago, yet God warns us of things we will begin to see in the last days. We are seeing all God's warning in plain view from Genesis to Revelations. The warnings are there; heed the warning and follow God's instructions.

Backdrop 55

God said He will remove our sins as far as the East is from the West (Psalms 103:12). God uses many illustrations and parables to help us understand His Word. I once thought "as far as the east is from the west" spoke of from one side of the map to the other. And with my thought process, from the east coast to the west coast is about 2,800 miles. When we think in reference of our sins, that's not very far. But there is always a word within the word of God.

While listening to Christian TV one day, without any effort on my part, this scripture was explained. If at any time you have trouble understanding God's Word, ask Him for understanding. It may not come in a matter of seconds, but it will come. God will speak directly to you through the Spirit or place someone in your path to help with your confusion.

Okay, back to the east coast, west coast. As I was watching, the minister explained we have a South Pole and a North Pole and distance can be measured but there is no West nor East pole.

As I continued to think about this even deeper, God began teaching me as well. He showed me that the east coast is bordered by the Atlantic Ocean and the west coast by the Pacific Ocean. Anyone who has ever stood on a shoreline, on a balcony overlooking the ocean or gone on a cruise, you cannot see an end to the ocean. If anyone sets out on a ship trying to find where the oceans end, it's a waste of time because there is no end.

Rhythm 55

East Coast, West Coast

As far as my eyes can see, my God watches over me.

Through dangers seen and unseen and all my mess in between, sometimes it's all my fault. I praise You for that halt of what the devil had planned for me, You had already seen.

And you made provision for me so that sin wouldn't follow me. You place Grace and Mercy on my track, and for this very reason, I won't turn back.

As far as the east is from the west, a sinful life is what I contest; Your word is oh so true; You made a way for the wrong I do.

But only if I confess and give you only my best, as far as the east is from the west, you remember not my sin and give me rest.

Stage Exit

It's amazing how far our wrongdoings are away from the thoughts of God; He is amazing. And only an amazing God can do such an amazing thing. "As far as the east is from the west, so far has he removed our transgressions from us (Psalm 103:12). Try to find an end to the ocean; it's not possible. Try to find an end to God's forgiveness; it's not possible. But remember: this isn't a license to sin.

Backdrop 56

Accounts of the Bible could sometimes have a person wondering, "How in the world could this be?"

One Sunday morning sermon by Pastor Vincent Riley put a little humor to one of Jesus's great miracles. What was said started my creative juices flowing and thinking about other accounts of the Bible that would have one thinking: "Wow, how did He do that?" or, "Really?" Well, with God, all things are possible, but sometimes…

Rhythm 56

This Makes No Sense...

56–1 (Genesis 17)

You promised a son to me; I really can't see how this could be. I'm almost a hundred years old, and most of my flare is gone.

But you say to me this day, a son is coming my way.

This makes no sense to me; my wife is as old as me.

To believe we will give birth to a son is far and beyond anything I can hope or think. Is this a prank?

God never goes back on a promise; Abraham yet again fathered a son in his old age; a miracle came his way.

56-2 (Luke 1:27–35)

God's angel appeared to me and in essence said, "You are a mother to be.

"You will give birth to the Son of God; Jesus is what He shall be called.

"It was prophesized He will be the One to reign for eternity, the true and begotten Son, born to a virgin; this must be done.

"He will save all who believe and willing to leave a life of sin behind and live for God for the rest of their lives."

"Do not be afraid," the angel said, "for your Son comes to save."

Such news I couldn't understand since I've never known a man. How could this possibly be? *This makes no sense to me.*

God did as the angel said. The virgin give birth and her Son led people willing to take up their cross, for we were all once lost.

56-3 (John 9)

I've been blind since the time of birth. Some questioned whether it was a curse.

They ask was it due to sin, from me or from my kin.

But Jesus spoke up and basically said, "It's neither of which you have said. It was to bring glory to the power of God, the reason why I was called."

So Jesus led the blind man away from the negativity onlookers would display.

When He had come to a certain place, He brought forth mercy and grace.

Then spitting on the ground, a mixture of mud was found to be a healing balm; I imagine no one remained calm.

Are you kidding me? This is how I will again see how could it be. *This makes no sense to me.*

But when all was said and done, the blind man saw the Son and began to praise God's name for his sight which he had gained.

56-4 (2 Kings 5)

I'm sick of this skin disease. I'm a mighty warrior; I should stand at ease.

But all I feel is pain, and such a disease could cause one much shame.

Then one day a young girl said, "I know of a man. Elisha is his name.

"He has the healing power of God, and you should give him a call." So I did as the young girl said and went in search of this man. Who could heal me of this disease, then I can stand at ease?

But the message that was sent to me: *this makes no sense to me.* I was told to go wash in the river; the thought of that made me quiver.

I became very angry that day and began to stalk away.

Rivers are in my hometown, and I've covered much ground to reach this healing man; and this is what he said:

"Go and wash yourself seven times in the Jordan River;"

You would think after all the gifts I delivered;

No one would ever consider telling me to do such a thing After all, I'm a friend of the king.

But as I stalked away, there was one who encouraged me that day

Advise I do as the prophet had said and put my pride away

Thank God for those who encouraged, the one who is discouraged, for on that very day, the mighty warrior's disease went away.

Stage Exit

God will, at times, require we do things that to us, just don't make sense. God may ask you give something to someone, and you wonder why. It's because that person has prayed for what God is asking you to give. Take some time to remember a time God asked you to give your time, money, or talents, and you will see, all was returned or it's on the way.

Are you all right with dying for your rights?

Paul said, "All things are lawful for me, but not all things are helpful; all things are lawful for me, but not all things edify" (1 Corinthians 10:23). When reading this passage of scripture, don't read what isn't there. I have a friend who says, "Don't hear what I am not saying." In other words, don't read this scripture and say, "I can steal, kill, and destroy because Paul said, 'All things are lawful' for me."

Let's take a few minutes to dissect what Paul is saying because I wouldn't want anyone to take scripture out of context.

> Behold, I set before you today a blessing and a curse: the blessing, if you obey the command-ments of the Lord your God which I command you today; and the curse, if you do not obey the commandments of the Lord your God, but turn aside from the way which I command you today, to go after other gods which you have not known. (Deuteronomy 11:26)

We have the right to make a choice between the blessing or the curse. God doesn't make us choose one or the other; we have the right to choose which we want.

What the scripture is not saying is this: we have the right to break the law(s) put before us. Anything that is within boundaries of the law or policies, we have the right to do. But everything we have the right to do by law isn't morally right to do. Got me?

For example, the First Amendment gives us freedom of speech; however, it doesn't mean we say things that tear down instead of building up and edify. The First Amendment also gives groups of people the right to assemble for that in which they believe. But if what we believe in is demeaning or degrading, is it morally right to assemble and express that belief?

You have the right to carry thousands of dollars in your purse or wallet. But if someone comes to you with a gun to take all your money away, are you going to refuse giving it up because it's your right to carry as much money as you want? Or are you going to give it up because what you have the right to do is not worth dying over?

You have the right to drink all the alcohol you want, but when that habit is destroying your life and the people around you, is that right worth losing everything, even your life?

You have the right to eat whatever you want, but when what you eat affects your health, is it worth it?

If you are of age, by law, you have the right to gamble all your money away. But when it destroys families, is it morally right?

During the civil rights movement, many stood up against what was lawfully right because it went against what was morally right. And there were loss of lives for what was lawfully right but morally wrong. These people knew standing up for what was morally right could cause them to lose their life, but they were all right with dying for the rights of themselves and others.

The bottom line is this: there are things in the world that can be done legally but still bring destruction to lives and can even cause death. So are you willing to die (physically or spiritually) for what is right by man's law but wrong by God's law? Or are you willing to do what the scripture says, "No greater love than this that a man would lay down his life for a friend"?

Backdrop 57

We have all been around the naysayers and those with negative opin-
ions. We also encounter people on our jobs that engage in gossip and
negative conversation. Some even try to bring others down to their
level. If you remember back in Rhythm 38, I am fascinated with
eagles. Eagles possess some habits, characteristics, and abilities we
should adopt in our human lifestyle.

Rhythm 57

I Fly Too High

I fly too high so thus I am free from negativity trying to touch me.

It stays on my track, trying to bring me back to a way of life that's full of strife.

But what negativity doesn't know is I have decided to let things go. And Neg, I will call, can plainly see, that I am happy and totally set free, but as we know, misery loves company.

And every time Neg comes my way, I do an about face and turn the other way.

I begin to fly a little higher, but here, Neg comes by my side, telling me this and complaining about that just like a monkey on my back.

Yet higher and higher, I continue to soar.

Negativity I will ignore.

I fly too high, so thus I am free; only God can touch me.

Don't get me wrong with what I just said, but negativity can't come my way.

I fly too high, and this you shall see; all that mess is far below me.

I fly too high please understand;

Negativity is not in my plan.

Stage Exit

Joel Osteen said, "You can't soar with the eagles if you are on the ground pecking with the chickens."

Backdrop 58

Bishop T.D. Jakes recorded a snippet sermon from one of his Woman Thou Art Loosed Conferences concerning the mind. In this short sermon, he tells how we often get sleep but not rest. It wasn't until I experienced such a situation for myself that I fully understood what he was saying.

While taking a nap one day, I had a dream. I was in the dream along with three other people. Three of us were in my car, and another person was trying to force their way in the car, but I kept fighting to keep this person out. Somehow, I was forced out of the car, and the other three drove off. I tried calling one of the three in the car but couldn't get through. My phone was cluttered with so much stuff until I couldn't get a call through. When I woke up from my dream, I was literally exhausted.

Rhythm 58

Battles in the Mind

My mindset can be like a maze; but my God is amazing!
Circumstances and situations play in my mind.
Making life seem so unkind.
I try to figure things out; trying to make sense of all the thoughts
that roam about in my mind that sometimes leave me confined.
To a place I wish not to be trapped in my own thinking; I'm no lon-
ger free.
Some situations and circumstances trouble me, causing confusion to
guide me.
My mindset can be like a maze; my God is a maze end.
His will is to transform me; His will is to renew me.
My mindset was like a maze; the word of God is amazing!

Stage Exit

God will keep us in perfect peace if we keep our mind stayed on
him (Isaiah 26:3).

A Blind Moment

For most of my adult Christian life, I have heard of Saul (Paul) traveling down the Damascus Road and how he was struck blind by the power of God. Saul was persecuting Christians, going to their homes and dragging away men and women who profess Jesus Christ as their Lord and Savior.

> As he journeyed, he came near Damascus, and suddenly a light shone around him from heaven. Then he fell to the ground, and heard a voice saying "Saul, Saul, why are you persecuting Me?" (Acts 9:3–4)

> Then Saul arose from the ground, and when his eyes were opened, he saw no one. But they led him by the hand and brought him into Damascus. (Acts 9:8)

When I first learned about Saul, later his name was changed to Paul, my interpretation of the scripture was, "God struck Saul blind, and for this reason he converted to a person preaching the Gospel of Jesus." I couldn't have been more wrong. Without even asking (if you remember, earlier I said, I often ask God for understanding of scripture), God spoke to me and said, "Saul didn't change because I struck him blind. Saul changed because his heart was changed."

And this is what we all must do: change our hearts. Have what God told me: "a blind moment."

> And he was three days without sight, and neither
> ate nor drank. (Acts 9:9)

A blind moment could be considered as a time when we close our eyes to things going on around us and see only God and His plans for our lives. The number three seem to have significance in the Bible. My Google research of the number three in the Bible states it represents divine wholeness, completeness, and perfection. The Trinity: God the Father, God the Son, and God the Holy Spirit—three. Jesus was in the grave for three days. God's attributes: omniscience, omnipresence, and omnipotence. And we could go on and on.

In three days, Saul (later Paul) changed his life for the better and lived for Jesus. We can do the same if we sit still and place our focus on God. He will not make us do anything. However, when we are heading in the wrong direction, God will stop us long enough so we can take the time to think about the path we are taking.

Backdrop 59

A scene in the movie *War Room* brought awareness to a challenge we at times face in life. The movie concerned a wife fighting to save her marriage and a husband who didn't seem to care. In one scene, Tony and his friend Mike are at the gym and they begin discussing giving CPR to someone in need. Mike told of a time he gave CPR to a woman in a restaurant who had garlic for dinner. Tony said he would not give CPR to anyone. Mike replies, "You're not going to just let someone die in front of you while you eat your salad."

Tony's reply was, "I don't do CPR, Mike. I'll just call 911."

Mike said, "That's just cold. You just going to let somebody die? What if it was your wife?" There was no reply from Tony. The awareness this scene brought to me was this: there are people in relationships that are hurting. For the most part, one is the hurter and one the hurt. One party or both at times will allow the relationship to be destroyed before admitting, "We should seek help." Think of it like this: you are drowning, and someone is standing nearby. Are you going to choose to drown, or are you going to yell with all your might, "Help!"

Rhythm 59

CPR: Covered Pride Revealed

You mean to tell me you would rather die?

My Brother, my Sister, that's dangerous pride.

To realize you need help, but you chose to cure yourself.

Pride can be a dangerous thing when it centers around personal gain.

Accomplishments, we all understand. But this thing is hard to comprehend.

It's a matter of dying to self instead of allowing pride to kill self. Or destroying those around you. My Brother, my Sister, I beseech you, let go of this foolish thing you do.

Lay self-righteousness aside; let go of your foolish pride.

Think about all you stand to lose.

It's about life, so please choose to redefine your CPR to Caring, Protecting, and Reviving.

Stage Exit

Hopefully we will exit this stage realizing, "We don't have it all together." Pastor Riley preached on the many faces we sometimes wear. It's time to come from behind the mask and say, "I need help. I can't do this on my own."

Backdrop 60

So much goes on in the spirit that we do not see. We pray for things to happen, and it takes longer than expected for God to give an answer. The book of Daniel 9–10 tells how Daniel prayed for his people because they had disobeyed God, again. All of Israel sinned greatly and were not following the voice of God as spoken by His prophets, again. Israel had become wicked and did evil in the sight of God, again. Despite all God had done to bring them out of the clutches of Pharaoh, they didn't follow God's commandments, again.

Daniel prayed to God for his people. He reminded God of how gracious and merciful He is and how, for this reason, Israel should be spared. In Daniel 9, the angel Gabriel spoke to Daniel concerning his prayers. In Daniel 10, the angel Michael came to help. At both times, Daniel is assured his prayers were heard. Gabriel explained how God heard him since the first time he prayed and sent him (Gabriel) to help.

Gabriel said, "For twenty-one days the spirit prince of the kingdom of Persia (an evil spirit) blocked my way. Then Michael, one of the archangels, came to help me, and I left him there with prince of the kingdom of Persia." In other words, Gabriel left Michael fighting with the evil spirit so that he could continue on to help Daniel.

Rhythm 60

I Heard You the First Time

I prayed, and I prayed for many days, asking God to take this away.
The hardship I endure, the pain I feel is far more than I care to bear.
What I didn't know and what I didn't see were thousands of angels
    watching over me.
Look into the atmosphere with your spiritual eyes; therein you will
    see angels by your side
Standing tall, swords drawn, thousands upon thousands conquering
    all.
So, hold your horses, slow your row, our God in heaven of course,
    He knows
Our hearts desires, that burning fire.
Those things we pray for; God's angels slay for
It's not based on our time, it's based on His.
It may seem like a long time, but He heard us the first time.

Stage Exit

Before we exit this stage, rest assured that God gives His angels
charge to protect us and fight for us in the unseen. You may say,
"Then why so much tragedy?" I don't claim to know all the answers.
I do know that God is still on the throne; He sees and knows all.

Forward Lean, Dream Keeper

The first Sunday of 2019, my pastor, Vincent Riley, preached a sermon titled "Catch Your Second Wind." He spoke of how we reach low points in life, but we must put ourselves in a place where we can "catch a second wind." Meaning, don't give up but regroup.

One illustration he used for catching your second wind was runners jumping hurdles. This prompted me to do research and even put other things in my spirit to speak on. In this journey called life, figuratively speaking, we face: bumps, potholes, and even spikes in the road. The enemy will put anything he can in the way to slow us down from reaching our destiny. But not all delays are enemy based. Sometimes it's us not doing what we know in our spirit is right. We also face valleys, mountains, and hurdles.

Let's begin with bumps and potholes in the road. You are driving along your merry way and suddenly hit a *bump* or *pothole* in the road. The maker of the road (let's say God) didn't put it there, but something malfunctioned (let's say the enemy) and caused a bump or a pothole. Whatever the reason, we shouldn't focus too much on that, but we know bumps and potholes slow us down and can even cause damage. So what we will focus on is getting back on track by getting anything damage fixed by the maker (let's still say God) and staying focused to avoid the bumps and potholes.

Then we have *spikes*. If you've ever driven through certain places such as parking garages, you know what I mean. Spikes are purposely placed on the ground to avoid a person from driving in the wrong direction.

If for some reason a person decides to drive against the spikes, you will find yourself with flat tires. Let's say, when we try to go against God's way, He will always have a way to stop us (the spikes) in our track and cause us to sit there (flat tires) and think about the wrong choice(s) we made.

Psalm 23 declares, "Yea though I walk through the *valley* of the shadow of death I will fear no evil for though are with me." Yes, we will have walks in life that feel like we are going to literally die. But remember, it's only a shadow and shadows can't hurt. Shadows reflect off the light (the Son of God). This scripture goes on to say that even with this walk, God is with us.

Moving on to the *mountains*. Mark 11:23 says, "Truly I tell you, if anyone says to this mountain, 'go, throw yourself into the sea,' and does not doubt in their heart but believes that what they say will happen, it will be done for them."

In my younger days, I enjoyed singing a popular Gospel song called "The Rough side of the Mountain." Pastors Melody and David Burford say, "The message is in the song." They adopted a way of life that I live by to this day. They do not sing songs just because it's tradition. Not to offend anyone, instead of climbing the rough side of the mountain, speak to that mountain and declare what Jesus told His disciples in Mark 11:23. He didn't tell them to climb the rough side of the mountain; He told them to have faith and command that mountain to move.

Now we come to the hurdles. The *hurdles* are what brought me here to begin with. In my research, I discovered there are types or leans to help a runner jump over hurdles. There is the minimal lean, the downward lean, and the forward lean. Using my sanctified imagination, my interpretation of each may be slightly different than what is already written.

Let's start with the minimal lean. *Webster's* definition of minimal is of a small amount, quantity, degree, or negligible. Negligible means so small or unimportant as to be not worth considering or insignificant. Well, the minimal lean may get us cross the hurdle, but because it's so small, we may miss out on our destiny. We should always aim to go above and beyond what is asked. Jesus said in

Matthew 5:41, "If someone ask you to go one mile, go with them two miles."

Secondly, let's take a look at the downward lean. Webster's definition of the word downward is moving or leading to a lower place or level. Okay, that move just doesn't work for me! My goal in life is to be all that God created me to be. He created us all to be the head and not the tail, above and not beneath, so that downward lean is not in my running game plan.

Lastly, we get to the forward lean which is the lean Pastor Riley recommends and the lean I choose to jump my hurdles with. *Webster*'s definition of the word forward is "in the direction that one is facing or traveling, toward the front, toward the future, onward (as in *Onward Christian Solider),* to make progress, ahead in time, looking forward, bold or familiar in manner, help to advance, promote, or move to a future destination."

The sport of track definition of forward lean is the hurdler does not duck his head down as in the downward lean; he keeps the chin up; the eyes are facing which he is moving toward the next hurdle toward the finish line. The leg must be lifted high off the ground and not lag as in the minimal lean.

According to "Hurdles First," the downward lean is the old school style of jumping. God says in Isaiah 43:19, "Behold, I will do a new thing; now it shall spring forth; shall ye not know it?" KJV

We will face difficult times. Stay focused, keep your head up, and move forward! Never give up on your dream(s). And always use a forward lean mind-set; dream keeper.

Backdrop 61

The Body

I am part of an awesome ministry: Meeting Place Church. God could not have put together a finer body of people: pastor, first lady, ministers, deacons, ushers, singers, and congregation. Our shepherd, Pastor Vincent Riley, is as David: "A Man after God's Heart."

Meeting Place is a church where we are family. You will never get lost in the crowd because we know each other by name, and we pray for each other.

While going through a spiritual storm one night, I was guided by so many members of the body, which led me to write this passage. I called out, and each one I called out to heard my cry and came running to my side at the speed of light. One minister said, "We are the body, and if one member of the body hurts, we all hurt." This statement is symbolic to the actual body. If your head hurts, it has an effect on the total body. Something as small as a toothache or a stumped toe affects the whole body—and with great pain, I must add.

We are the body of Christ. Our hands should be reaching out to people, to heal and to comfort. Our legs and feet should be moving toward people and seeking the lost to lead them to the cross. Our hearts should be compassionate so that we are sending a godly signal to our brains to speak life and not death to the body of Christ.

Rhythm 61

In the darkest hours of my night, I totally lost my sight. My spirit became weak indeed. I found myself on my knees, praying for Jesus to intercede. I called out to the body of Christ; in my darkest hour, they heard my plight. As Aaron and Hur stood by Moses, they held me up; now I can tell the story. The body connected in such a way and stopped what they were doing to pray; my discouragement went away; I was encouraged from that very day.

Stage Exit

How wonderful is the body of Christ. It's awesome to have those you can call and say a simple "Pray for me." And it is equally important that you be a member of the body of Christ for those in need.

Backdrop 62

Pay It Forward

The saying goes, "There is nothing new under the sun." A trend is sweeping the nation called "Pay it forward." I can proudly say I have reaped from and sowed into this concept. It's awesome to know in a world where so many people do cruel acts that there is still kindness. Pay it forward covers the debt of the person that is to come after you. Chances are the sower of pay it forward doesn't know the reaper, but their hearts were pricked to do a kind deed. While reflecting on this trend one morning, it reminded me of the ultimate pay it forward started by Almighty God through His Son, Jesus, over two thousand years ago. Jesus paying a debt He didn't owe was the true beginning of "Pay it forward."

Rhythm 62

Before we were formed in the womb, God's Love consumed (Jeremiah 1:5).

Before the chapters of our lives began, God had an awesome plan (Jeremiah 29:11).

Before we were given a name, God made a trade for our shame (Romans 10:11).

Before we made a choice, God gave His voice (Deuteronomy 30:19).

Before we made our first mistake, God made provisions for our sake (Genesis 3).

Before we shed our first tear, God said, "Be of good cheer" (John 16:33).

Before we felt any pain, God broke every chain (Galatians 5:1).

And before there was loss, God paid the cost (Mark 10:45).

Stage Exit

Be kind and give of your money, time, and talents. God will restore all that you do in His name.

These Simple Words

Life lessons can be learned through everyday living if we take the time to listen and learn. And the ones who teach these lessons are everyday people like Deacon Thomas Hicklin. I never had the pleasure of meeting Deacon Hicklin, but I met his beautiful wife, the late Mother Lucille Hicklin and most of his children and grandchildren. I was told Deacon Hicklin was a man of little words, but when he spoke, you best to have listened because what he had to say was profound.

I attended the home-going service of Deacon Hicklin and listened to all the wonderful things people had to say about him. One statement has stuck with me to this very day, and I will forever keep it in my spirit. (Sidebar: it's so important to keep God's word and godly wisdom in our spirits. Our flesh and our minds will sometimes fail us, but a godly spirit will never fail us.)

A gentleman stood and shared a memory of Deacon Hicklin. He told how he was at church one day looking for something in frustration but couldn't find what he was looking for. Deacon Hicklin noticed him and said these simple words, "Maybe you're not looking for the right thing."

One may say, "What's so profound about that?"

Well, I'm glad you ask because I'm more than happy to tell you.

We must have a mind and spirit willing to hear God's people speaking. It may seem as though what is said is menial when in fact, it can be life changing. In life, we spend so much time frantically searching for things. We can look at this from two sides: physical things and spiritual things.

Although this gentleman was looking for something physical, I perceived Deacon Hicklin's statement was spiritual.

When looking for something physical or tangible, sometimes if we just sit down and calm down, we will find what we are looking for. Sometimes, we can simply say, "Lord, help me find it."

But it is my perception that Deacon Hicklin went to a deeper level: the spiritual. This is what my spirit fed off his statement. We spend so much time, effort, and energy looking for things that don't even matter. How much greater would our lives be if we took that same time, effort, and energy and put it into seeking the kingdom of God? Matthew 6:33 says, "But *seek* ye first the kingdom of God and his righteousness, and all these things will be added to you."

The Bible doesn't say some things; it said all things. That could be something as simple as looking (seeking) for car keys. It doesn't matter; God is a present help in all areas of our lives.

It's not necessary to say a lot to mean a lot. These simple words will impact my life forever!

Backdrop 63

Faith

Faith is essential for serving God.

> But without faith it is impossible to please Him. (Hebrews 11:6)

> By faith Abraham, when called to go to a place he would later receive as his inheritance, obeyed and went even though he did not know where he was going. (Hebrews 11:8)

> By faith Noah, when warned about things not yet seen, in holy fear built an ark to save his family. (Hebrews 11:7)

> I tell you; I have not found such great faith not even in Israel. (Luke 7:9)

We should all be familiar with scriptures speaking on faith. One of my favorite is found in Matthew 15:28: "Jesus said, 'Dear woman your faith is great. Your request is granted.'"

Rhythm 63

Jesus arrived in a certain city one day
A Canaanite woman came his way
Begging and pleading, "Have mercy on me.
My daughter is possessed by a demon."
But Jesus spoke not a word.
It was as if her pleas weren't heard.
Now, his disciples were disturbed
Because Jesus said not a word
"Tell her to go away"
"She is bothering us with this display."
But the woman continued to speak.
Jesus replied, "I was sent only to God's lost sheep."
It's not fitting to take from God's children
Then give it to the dogs.
The Canaanite women didn't stop; she continued her dialogue,
"Lord, I know this is true
"But this I say to you
"Crumbs that fall from the masters table; even the dogs have favor."
Jesus moved by compassion, was pleased with this woman's faith.
And from that very moment, her daughter's demons went away.

Stage Exit

Faith is the cornerstone of the Christian world. Without faith,
it is impossible to please God.

Backdrop 64

Quite often, I find myself in a mess, but I have also learned, a mess can be the beginning of a great message. When we are transparent and honest, we can do great works for the kingdom of God.

Rhythms 64

This Thing
(Inspired by Minister Bryan Hardy)

This thing I'm going through is filled with so much stress; so I was
on my way to do my mess
God stopped me; remember, it's only a test
This thing I'm going through makes me angry indeed; I was on the
way to plant that bitter seed
God stopped me; remember, I Am is all you need
This thing I'm going through makes me wanna scream; my outlook,
this thing is extreme
God stopped me; remember, in your eye is also a beam (Matthew
7:5, KJV)
This thing I'm going through makes me upset; I am about to say or
do things I will soon regret
God stopped me; remember, don't fret.
This thing I'm going through makes it hard to perceive; the plan the
Good Father has for me.
But His word is truth; He always comes through.

I am on the way to do my message; it's filled with love and godly
lessons.

Stage Exit

I've heard it said, "If you haven't been through hard times then just keep on living, baby." Things won't always go according to our plan(s). But God has truly been my rock. And godly friends also helps.

Even Faith Gets Tired Sometimes

I was inspired to write these words of encouragement during a Sunday morning sermon by Pastor Vincent Riley after his statement, "Even faith gets tired."

Until that day, I never thought of faith as getting tired. Matthew 17:20 states, "Because you have so little faith. Truly I tell you, if you have faith as small as a mustard seed, you can say to this mountain, 'Move from here to there,' and it will move. Nothing will be impossible for you."

A mustard seed is 1–2 milliliters in size. If you've ever had a betta fish, the food bettas eat is very small. A mustard seed is about the size of one beta bite. So you would think with something that small having faith would be a breeze. Well, for some of us, that's not the case. If we are honest, things get hard and our faith gets a little shaky. It's nothing to be ashamed of. It doesn't mean we lose our salvation nor does it mean we have no faith. It simply means we are as Proverbs 13:12 says, "Hope deferred makes the heart sick." Hope is having faith in what we want to see in our lives.

Abraham is the father of faith, but even he had doubts when God spoke to him concerning being a father of many nations.

> "And I will bless her and give you a son from her!"
> Then Abraham bowed down to the ground, but he laughed to himself in disbelief. "How could I become a father at the age of 100? And how can Sarah have a baby when she is ninety years old?" (Genesis 17:16–17)

Does this scripture mean Abraham is no longer the father of faith? Does it mean he no longer has faith? He is one hundred, and Sarah, his wife, is ninety, well past her childbearing days. They both gave up on that dream of having children. They started off with faith because of God's promise: "Look up into the sky and count the stars if you can. That's how many descendants you will have!" Is this a contradiction between the Bible stating, "Abraham is the father of faith" and Abraham questioning, how could he and his wife have a baby in their old age? No, its faith grown tired.

Mark 9:24 tells of a father with a son possessed by evil spirits. The father explained to Jesus's disciples that when this evil spirit takes over his son, it won't let him talk and throws him violently to the ground. He went on to explain how he foams at the mouth, grinds his teeth, and at times the spirit throws him into fire and water trying to kill him. The disciples were unable to heal the boy, so they brought the boy to Jesus.

The father said, "Have mercy on us and help us, if you can." Jesus replied, "What do you mean, 'If I can.' Anything is possible if a person believes." Then the father said, "I do believe but help me overcome my unbelief" (Mark 9:24)?

Sounds like a contradiction on behalf of the Father, huh? These episodes were happening since this man's son was a boy. The Bible doesn't give an age of the son at the time he went to Jesus. I would guess this was an adult son since the father stated, "Since he was a boy." I would say, the answer to the question at hand is "No, it's not a contradiction. It's faith that's grown tired."

Sisters Mary and Martha sent for Jesus when their brother Lazarus was sick and dying, but Jesus didn't come right away. In fact, by the time He arrived, Lazarus had been dead four days. John 11:21 states, "Martha said to Jesus 'Lord, if only you had been here, my brother would not have died. But even now I know that God will give you whatever you ask.'"

Even after the death of Lazarus, Martha had faith that her brother Lazarus would live again, not on earth but in heaven. Does this mean she stopped having faith because Jesus didn't come when they thought He would? Does this mean they stopped having faith after Lazarus died? No, this means their faith grew tried waiting on Jesus.

This is what happens to many believers. God doesn't answer as quickly as we want, thus our faith grows tired. But remember the saints of old, "He may not come when we want but he'll be there right on time." God's timing is not our timing, and His ways are not our ways; but trust and believe He loves us and will never leave nor forsake us.

Backdrop 65

Step-by-step is not just a cliché; it's a way of life. In fact, it's God's way of life. While reading Joyce Meyer's *Healing the Soul of a Woman,* one scripture reference comes from Genesis 1–3. As I begin to meditate on those chapters, I heard God say, "Step-by-step."

Rhythm 65

Step-by-Step

Step-by-step is what it takes to travel through life; those were the words I heard God say.

Since the beginning of time this I say, step-by-step; earth was created this very way.

In His infinite wisdom and His awesome power, day one was created; light overpowered; the darkness that formed, light made it become day; the lesser light, God called it night.

Step-by-step is what it takes to travel through life, I heard God say.

In His infinite wisdom and His awesome power, day two was created; the firmament divided, waters under and waters above from evening to morn; heaven is born!

Step-by-step is what it takes to travel through life, I heard God say.

In His infinite wisdom and His awesome power, day three was created; land yielding a harvest.

Grass and herbs, luscious fruit trees, God planted for us to provide our need.

Step-by-step is what it takes to travel through life, I heard God say.

In His infinite wisdom and His awesome power, day four was created; the firmament divided, day and night is what we have, and beautiful sights gave us light.

The lesser light given, the stars and the moon. The brighter light given; the sun illumes.

Step-by-step is what it takes to travel through life, I heard God say.

In His infinite wisdom and His awesome power, day five was created, ground creature and fowl. From land to sea, there came to be, creatures that walked and some swam the seas.

Step-by-step is what it takes to travel through life, I heard God say.

In His infinite wisdom and His awesome power, day six was created; creatures have power to produce after his kind, and God saw that it was good but this God clearly understood, the need for a creature to be created as Himself, so in his own image a spirit is born, having dominion over the earth, man, God's son.

Step-by-step, I tell you it's true, it's the only way we will see it through.

In His infinite wisdom and His awesome power, day seven was created; God rest in His power. He set aside the seventh day for man to rest from prior days.

Stage Exit

As we exit this stage, do you get the point? God has the power to do all things. I believe everything He created in six days, He had the power to speak it all into existence at once. Yet He didn't create the earth all at once. He did it step-by-step, day by day. If God took the time, how much more should we?

Backdrop 66

Before the mid-1980s, cars were made from metal and not plastic. Back in the day, a wrecked car could survive (praise God for all those who survived) a collision. But nowadays, if you hit your car with a nerf ball, it causes a dent. And lo and behold, if you are involved in an accident, the assessor may say, "Total loss." Now, you are standing there looking at your insurance adjuster, scratching your head thinking, "What in the world! Are you telling me this is a total loss? It was barely hit!"

Rhythm 66

Total Loss

I don't always travel the direction God instructs me to go; as a result, I hit bumps in the road.

Breaking my spirit, messing with my mind.

Not following God's direction leaves me spiritually blind.

I didn't take the time to consider the cost.

Thank God He doesn't see a total loss.

I was traveling too fast, didn't take the time to cast; all my cares on the One who cares.

I carried a load; I lost control, got off track; the enemy on my back. Damage was done; God sent His Son to bear a cross because He didn't see a total loss.

Stage Exit

We exit this stage knowing, no matter how damaged we are, God is the ultimate fixer.

Mount Up!

One morning, after dropping my son off at school, I was listening to a broadcast of Family Talk featuring CrossHope Ministries. The minister spoke of difficult things people face but quite often keep those things inside. He mentioned many members in his church were facing difficult times and how he had no knowledge of this until someone on his staff brought it to his attention.

He based his teachings on Psalms 55. The scripture speaks of troubles King David faced and how he cried out to God. David, as he was called "a giant slayer, a mighty king, a man after God's own heart," was so overwhelmed with troubles until in Psalms 55, he said, "Fear and trembling overwhelm me, and I can't stop shaking. Oh, that I had wings like a dove; then I would fly away and rest!"

Most of the book of Psalms was written by David. It was written during times of grief, fear, feeling lonely, or depressed.

I can remember times of uncertainty in my life, dark places. And it was during those times I wished I could fly away from it all. God tells us to mount up as wings of an eagle (Isaiah 40:31, KJV) but I have learned, He didn't say this for us to fly away from what troubles us. How do I know this, you ask? I know this because He showed it to me in his word. Keep reading...

"But they that wait upon the LORD shall *renew their strength*; they shall mount up with wings as eagles; they shall run, and *not be weary*; and they shall walk and *not faint*." (Isaiah 40:31)

Let's pay close attention to this scripture. Until I wrote this passage, I never noticed what the scripture is truly saying. It's not telling us to fly; the scripture clearly states, "They shall RUN and not be weary. They shall WALK and not faint." Obviously, during these troubled times, we aren't flying; we are still on the ground. Still in the midst of it all (running the course and walking through it or walking it out) *but*, at the same time, we are mounting up.

The dictionary defines the word mount as climb upstairs, a hill, or other rising surfaces, or to ascend. It is my belief that mount up is symbolic to renewing the spirit and the mind. We are preparing ourselves with the mind-set of flying above all that troubles us. We are climbing higher; we are ascending.

As it's been said many times before, we all go through difficult times in life, and as the minister of CrossHope Ministries said, it's vital to not keep these things inside. There will be times when we need others to help us mount up.

Yes, God is an ever-present help. He will never leave us nor forsake us, but there are times when we need that human touch. There are times when we need someone to help us mount up when we don't have the strength to do it alone. I can honestly say, if it wasn't for the encouragement of relatives and friends, I don't know where I would be.

With reading scriptures from the book of Psalms, King David faced many difficult times. And we will face difficult times as well. Depression is sweeping the world at alarming rates. There is nothing new under the sun, and if we take the time to read God's Word, we will find a cure for what troubles our mind and our spirit.

Mount up as wings of an eagle and soar above all your troubles.

Backdrop 67

I have heard this phrase several times: "You may be the only Bible some people will ever see/read." Keeping this in mind, we must be careful of how we treat people. God loves us all regardless of the mistakes we make. He doesn't see anyone as better than another. Therefore, the words "I'm better than you" should never flow out of our mouths. We may make better choices than others but should *never* see ourselves as better than *anybody*!

Rhythm 67

Sunday Morning

It's Sunday morning; praise and worship is high. A newcomer walks in, also high. The clothes are wrinkled, and the smell is strong. You can tell this newcomer partied all night long. The greeter ushers the newcomer to a seat, not as welcoming as a greeter should be. The stares and the whispers are obviously loud. The reactions can be seen without a doubt. But what isn't known under the wrinkled clothes is this newcomer has decided, it's time to build an eternal home. But this newcomer has never accepted Jesus in their life and decided this day, "I will give Him a try." The stares and the glares turn the newcomer away; the newcomer turns around and walks away. One lost sheep headed out the door; the newcomer decides not to answer the knock at the door.

    It's Sunday morning; praise and worship is high. A newcomer walks in, dress so high; it's cut very low; the heels also high; you can tell by her style she walks many miles. The greeter ushers her to a seat, placing her in a corner, to keep her discreet. But eyes are focused on the newcomer's style; the perspective of her is she is wild. But what isn't known and what isn't seen is that underneath the perfume and oil sheen, she has searched and searched for someone to love her—someone who doesn't want anything in return from her. The stares and the glares are more than she can bear; she gets out her seat, not so discreet, and decides to leave this unwelcoming scene; she walks outside and down the street; she approaches the first man that she meets. Another lost sheep walks out the church door and answers the knock at the door no more.

It's Sunday morning; praise and worship is high. A newcomer walks in, children by her side. Not one, but two, and from what I can see, at any given day comes baby number three. Another single mom, as far as the eye can see because a ring on her finger, none to see. The mom is seated out of view; she feels rejected and abandoned too. She looks around and as far as she can see, "the congregation doesn't even see me." She gets up abruptly, her children by her side; holding their hands, she leads them outside. More lost sheep walk out the door; this single mom answers the knock no more.

It's Sunday morning; praise and worship is high. A newcomer walks in; is he purified? Tattoo after tattoo is all that can be seen; so many piercings. How it could be that he dare walks in the church of God? The Old Testament said, it's not accepted at all. The stares and the glares made the newcomer scared; he shies away from church that day. But what the church failed to realize that day was grace and mercy took the law away. And once again, on that day, another lost sheep remains astray.

Stage Exit

How we live our lives may be as close as some will ever come to know Jesus!

Backdrop 68

Experience teaches us that everything doesn't come to us as we expect it to. So many blessings are missed in life because we are looking for it one specific way, but remember, "God's way is not our way."

Rhythm 68

He Came a Different Way
(Inspired by Pastor Vincent Riley)

From beginning to the end, He came a different way. This was proclaimed by God's angel one day. Appearing to Mary, engaged to Joseph, a virgin she was; here is the story. The angel Gabriel announced, "And it's true. A king of the world shall be born from you."

But this confused Mary for this she knew. "A virgin I am, how could this be true?"

Then Gabriel explained, "This shall be. Listen to the word which comes from me. The Holy Spirit will come upon you. The power of the Most High will overshadow you. You will give birth to the Son of God. Holy and righteous, the world will stand in awe."

This I say, He came a different way; born King of the Jews in a stable one day. No pillow, no bed which to lay His head, wrapped in swaddling clothing, in a manger He laid.

This I say, He came a different way; at the age of twelve astonishing the crowd one day. He lingered behind; His parents were desperate to find where Jesus had strayed; He was missing that day. Three long days they searched for the Son, finding Him in the Temple the people were stunned.

Jesus Christ, our Lord and our King, walked this earth among mere men. A king you say, how could this be? A king you say walked with the common like me? Yes, it's true because He loves you; this I say, He came a different way.

This I say, He came a different way, riding on a donkey through the town one day. Is this the man you say is a king? Is this the man who's said to reign? Kings ride upon stallions or sit in golden chariots. This king, I say, came a different way.

Stage Exit

We shouldn't go through life thinking things can only come by a certain way. A homeless person on the street could one day be a great minister of the Gospel.

Delight Yourself!

Reading and understanding scripture is vital for our Christian walk. I can remember in my early days of this journey, I would read my Bible according to a "read your Bible in a year" chart. I made it all the way to mid-July one year and realized I had no idea what I read the months prior. I began to think what a shame and a waste to spend time reading my Bible daily and not remember anything I've read. At that point, I began to concentrate on reading for knowledge, wisdom, understanding, and revelation opposed to how many books of the Bible I have under my belt, so to speak. Once I began reading for understanding, God opened a world of revelation knowledge, and I am so grateful He took the time to slow me down.

I have many favorite scriptures. The one I like to share now is Psalms 37:4 (NLT): "Take delight in the Lord, and he will give you your heart's desire." I read this scripture and thought, "Yes! All I need to do is read my Bible, pray, and give God praise and what I want He will grant."

Not! It wasn't until recently that God gave me revelation knowledge of this scripture in my life. Someone else may see it differently, but this is what God showed me: what I thought was my desire wasn't.

Another scripture is Matthew 6:33 (NLT), which says, "Seek the Kingdom of God above all else, and live righteously, and he will give you everything you need." Both scriptures, Psalms 37:4 and Matthew 6:33, let us know, when we delight ourselves in the Lord, He will give us our desires and what we need.

But guess what? Come close and listen very carefully because what I didn't know was this: He will put a desire in our hearts! Whoa!

We may think this or that is our desire, but I am living proof of what I thought was my desire, for over twenty-eight years, wasn't. When I realized this, it was like, "Oh my God!" I can't believe I was so ignorant as to not know the desires of my heart. And yes, I said ignorant. Paul tells us in 1 Thessalonians 4:13 and 1 Corinthians 12:1, that he would not have us to be ignorant, therefore he ministered knowledge to the people. How crazy was that? It's my heart, for crying out loud. I should know better than anyone what my desire is, but I didn't. Thus, we have: "He knows us far better than we know ourselves." (Romans 8:27 MSG)

I enjoy writing poems. I have friends and relatives that published books prior to mine. I made a promise to myself at the beginning of 2018 that I would complete my book of poetry by the end of that year. I accomplished what I purposed in my heart to do (my unknown heart's desire). Now, outside of God, family, and church, writing is all I want to do! And this is the desire of my heart: to become a well-known author. William McDowell said it best, "My life is not my own." So for future reference, just say, "God, what do I desire in life?" then wait for the good, good Father to answer.

Backdrop 69

God is a loving, merciful, and forgiving God. He is the giver of life, health, strength, and prosperity, just to name a few. But that doesn't mean we sit back with our arms folded and legs crossed waiting to receive. In such a position, we are powerless to do anything.

Rhythm 69

But First

There is nothing that we need that God won't supply…
But first, we must seek His Kingdom and His righteousness.
There is no sickness nor sorrow that God cannot heal…
But first, we must believe in the strips His Son bore for us.
There is nothing that can rob us of our peace…
But first, we must keep our minds stayed on Him.
There is nothing too hard for God to do…
But first, we must have faith the size of a mustard seed.
There is no situation too difficult for God…
But first, we must trust God and lean not on our own understanding.
There is nothing we shall desire in our hearts that God won't give
    us…
But first, we must delight ourselves in Him.
There is no dream too hard for God to make a reality…
But first, we must write the vision and make it plain.
There is no wickedness in the land that God cannot make righteous…
But first, we must turn from our wicked ways and seek His face.
There is no household that will be destroyed by the enemy…
But first, when He stands at the door knocking, we must let Him in.

Stage Exit

We don't get the privilege to live this Christian life all willy-nilly and fancy free; there is more that God requires of us.

Backdrop 70

God will speak to you in the midnight hours and dry every tear that falls from your eyes. He speaks through hurt and pain. He will comfort and give you peace; He will cuddle you in His arms and rock you to sleep.

Rhythm 70

Jesus the Man, Jesus the Christ

"What a Man, what a Man, what a Man, what a mighty good Man?"
The best I will ever have. He listens to me and never interrupts.
When feelings of loneliness start to creep in, He taps me and says, "I
Am with you always."

When I feel I'm at my wits end, He reminds me He is never-ending.
When I'm ready to give up, He reminds me of everything He gave
up.
When I'm at my lowest point, His empty grave reminds me, He went
even lower.
In my darkest times when it looks as if the sun will never shine, I'm
reminded He is the light; He is the Son rise.
He is my Beginning and my Ending, and He covers everything in
the middle.

Stage Exit

Jesus is the answer for what troubles us today.

True Love Stories

Greater love has no one than this, than to
lay down one's life for his friend.

—John 15:13 (NKJV)

In John, chapter 15, there are verses of Jesus speaking to His disciples about love and keeping His commandments. Jesus tells His disciples, "As the Father love Me, I also have loved you; abide in my love." There is no greater example of one laying down His life for His friends than what Jesus Christ did on the cross. The following passages are examples of true unselfish love, the kind of love that Jesus speaks of in John 15.

Charlotte, N.C., 1999: a young woman eight months pregnant was shot four times. Miraculously, she called 911 for help. As she struggled to provide details to the 911 operator, her main concern is that of her unborn child. Her son survived; unfortunately, she died a short while afterward.

Charlotte, N.C., 2006: a young mother to be, twenty-seven years old, decided to undergo cancer treatments after the birth of her son. She gave birth by caesarean section. Her son survived; unfortunately, she died shortly after the birth of her son.

Charlotte, N.C., 2014: an eleven-year-old boy jumped into a creek to save his seven-year-old sister's life. His sister survived; unfortunately, he died.

Chester, S.C., 2015: while waiting at a bus stop, an eleven-year-old boy pushed his sister out of the way when a car veered toward them. His sister survived; unfortunately, he died.

Charlotte, N.C, 2019: a gunman opened fire on students in a classroom at the University of North Carolina (UNCC). Two lives were lost, but due to the heroic actions by one of those lives, it resulted in many more being saved.

I know there are many more true love stories across the world, but these are a few of the ones I am aware of.

Backdrop 71

One of the most powerful statements I've ever heard during this journey called life was quoted by Todd White as he gave his testimony on *Praise the Lord.* He spoke of his many addictions and how he, at one point, was ready to end his life.

Todd White told the story of how he was on his way to the gun cabinet but stopped and opened a telephone book. Amazingly, the phonebook opened to a list of several churches. He chose one and went to that church. Once there, he met and began talking to a man at this church, telling this man everything that was wrong with his life. Todd then repeats what the man at church said to him: "Since you don't want your life, why not give it to someone who does?"

Todd replied, "Dude, who would want my life?"

The man answered, "Jesus would want your life."

Rhythms 71

My Life

If you think that life is not worth living, think of everything God
    has given:

His sunrise in early morning
His beautiful sunsets in the evening
His moon that shines at night
His stars that tinkle so bright
His breeze that rustle through the trees
Birds that sing as they proclaim spring
The ocean's water that roars as it approach the shore
Cool crisp water springs that leaves us thirsty for more
Mountain peaks so high, looking as if they will touch the sky
Valleys that stoop down oh so low, catching every bit of winter's first
    snow
And I would be remiss if I didn't say
He gives oxygen to the living every day

If you think that life is not worth living, think of everything God
    has given:
His word He gave us manifested into flesh
His Son He gave us; our present help

Liberty He gave us; His Son paid the price
So, man, woman, and child could have everlasting Life
The Sonrise He gave us early one Sunday morning!
The Sonrise He gave us in all His glory!

Stage Exit

No matter what you see as wrong in your life, give it to Jesus, and He will make it right.

Backdrop 72

Spanking a child may be painful to a parent (as well as the child) but necessary. Proverbs 13:24 states, "Those who spare the rod of discipline hate their children. Those who love their children care enough to discipline them." It may be painful for a parent to tell a child, "No, you aren't allowed to go there, or you aren't allowed to do this." It may be that we heard a small voice inside that drove us to this conclusion. We can't explain to our child(ren) why; possibly this is where the term "because I said so" comes from. Saying no may be painful, but for the protection of our child(ren), it is necessary.

Rhythm 72

I was inspired to write this poem after listening to the testimony of former NFL player Tommie Harris as he told of the loss of his wife.

Painful but Necessary

Abraham was forced to send his son away
I imagined his heart was vexed that day
He clung tightly to Ishmael;
looked at Hagar with compassion
Sarah his wife said this must happen
And although Abraham didn't agree
It was God the Father that gave comfort to his grief
Painful as it was to send his son astray
Necessary it was; God's plan is the better way
A treacherous leader rose in the land
He sent out a cruel and disheartening command
Kill all the male babies as soon as they are born
But the midwives feared God; the Hebrews grew strong
Another command came concerning boys that were born
Throw them into the river; they shall not live on!
But one special boy born during this time
Was saved by his mother, hidden from evil's sight
When she could no longer hide the babe
She came up with a plan and then she prayed
Painful as it was, she placed him in the river
Necessary it was; for he would be the one to deliver

King David did wrong in the sight of the Lord
And to King David a son was born
Because his deed which left God displeased
The child feel ill no medicine could ease
The babe of this illness so David mourned
And begged the Lord to save his son
Painful as it was to see his son pass away
Necessary it was David humbled himself that day
We needed a Savior to redeem us from sin
God created Jesus; our salvation begins
Jesus walked this earth, blameless in God's sight
Jesus walked this earth to give eternal life
Painful as it was to lay His life away
Necessary it was Jesus is the only way

Stage Exit

Life is not a bed of fresh cut roses. We endure emotional and physical pain which at times deemed to be necessary. Remember, God is a present help and is with us even until the ends of the earth (Matthew 28:20).

Mountaintop Experience

My dear brothers and sisters, at some point in our lives, we should have a mountaintop experience.

> Now it doesn't matter now. It really doesn't matter what happens now. I left Atlanta this morning and as we got started on the plane there were six of us. The pilot said over the public address system "we are sorry for the delay, but we have Dr. Martin Luther King on the plane and to be sure that all of the bags were checked and to be sure that nothing would be wrong on the plane we had to check out everything carefully. And we had the plan protected and guarded all night."
>
> Then I got into Memphis and some begin to say the threats or talk about the threats that were out of what would happen to me from some of our sick white brothers. Well, I don't know what will happen now. We've got some difficult days ahead, but it really doesn't matter with me now because I've been to the mountaintop. (Dr. Martin Luther King Jr. April 3, 1968, Mason Temple (COGIC), Memphis TN)

The famous, "I've Been to the Mountaintop" was the last speech given by Dr. King before he was assassinated. What many people may not know is this: Dr. King was not feeling well the night he gave his speech. He was physically and mentally exhausted. He stayed back at the hotel while his friends went on to the church because of his scheduled appearance.

There was a storm that night. The crowd had weathered the storm to see and hear Dr. King speak. Seeing their dedication and determination to hear and support Dr. King, Ralph Abernathy called Dr. King and asked him to come out to the church. Despite how poorly he felt, Dr. King agreed and arrived at the church one and half hours late to deliver his speech.

Dr. King went on to say,

> Like anybody, I would like to live a long life. Longevity has its place. But I'm not concerned about that now. I just want to do God's will. And He's allowed me to go up to the mountain. And I've looked over. And I've seen the Promised Land. I may not get there with you. But I want you to know tonight, that we, as a people, will get to the Promised Land! And so, I'm happy, tonight. I'm not worried about anything. I'm not fearing any man! Mine eyes have seen the glory of the coming of the Lord!

It is said that Dr. King predicted his own death. He stated, "I would like to live a long life. Longevity has its place. But I'm not concerned about that now."

I said all that to say this: the mountaintop experience I am speaking of is not death of life but death of situations and circumstances. If you are in the boat with me, it's time to let some things die in our lives. Again, this is not a physical death but the death of mind-sets (I'm going to do things my way), history and habits (this is how I've always done it), disappointments and hurts (I refuse to forgive and forget), and even some relationships must die.

One aspect of a mountaintop experience is dying to self. "I have been crucified with Christ; it is no longer I who live, but Christ lives in me; and the life which I now live in the flesh I live by faith in the

Son of God, who loved me and gave Himself for me" (Galatians 2:20, NKJV).

Once we die to self, God can then begin the process of taking us to the mountaintop so that we will see the Promised Land.

"Then Moses climbed Mount Nebo from the plains of Moab to the top of Pisgah, across from Jericho. There the Lord showed him the whole land" (Deuteronomy 34:1, NIV). The land God showed Moses was the Promised Land.

The land God has promised us (peace, joy, happiness, good health, prosperity, true friendships, godly marriages, dreams coming into existence, etc.) we must let go of certain things in our lives. Reason: sometimes we must travel light, no extra baggage. The more baggage we carry, the longer the journey, the harder it is to soar to the top of the mountain and see our promised land.

- "Well, I don't know what will happen now" (Ecclesiastes 8:7, NIV; since no one knows the future, who can tell someone else what is to come?).
- "We've got some difficult days ahead" (2 Timothy 3:1, MSG; don't be naïve. There are difficult times ahead).
- But it really doesn't matter with me now (I have learned to be content whatever the circumstances; Philippians 4:11, NIV).
- Because I've been to the mountaintop (Revelation 21:1; Then I saw a new heaven and a new earth).

When we get to the point of looking at that person and truly say, "I forgive you" or "I forgive me," when we truly get to the point of saying, "Not my will but Yours be done, Father," we have made it to the mountaintop and our promised land is in plain view, it's a matter of walking into it.

Backdrop 73

Matthew 13:58 gives an account of how Jesus went to His hometown, but because of the faith in the people there, many miracles were not done. Jesus is God in the flesh. His purpose was to give abundant and everlasting life. It's hard to believe that people choose not to accept the gift Jesus offers. The same can be said in our everyday lives. There are people that God placed in our path to help guide us along the way. Sadly, not everyone recognized this, and many forfeit the blessings of God.

Rhythm 73

Even Jesus

Even Jesus, the one who turned water into wine
That same Jesus opened the eyes of the blind
Even Jesus, who commanded the mute to talk
That same Jesus summoned the lame to walk
Even Jesus, who calmed the waters
That same Jesus walked on the waters
Even Jesus, who healed the sick
That same Jesus transformed the lunatic
Even Jesus, who lived without strife
That same Jesus brought the dead to life
Even Jesus, who prayed for the shrewd
That same Jesus fed a multitude
Even Jesus, who preached to thousands each day
That same Jesus had no place to stay
But what I find so hard to perceive: in his hometown were many that
     didn't believe
And so, it came that day, Jesus the Miracle Worker was turned away.
The people allowed their hearts to be hardened
This same Jesus decided to pardon
Then shaking the dust off His heel
For that reason, many were not healed.

Stage Exit

This scene brought great sadness to me because many didn't recognize the hand of God and was deprived of bright futures and great blessings. Remember: die to flesh and accept what God hands to us on golden platters.

Backdrop 74

God makes things plain for us to see. Some things are unknown, and some things we have no answer for; nevertheless, He is a Jeremiah 29:11 kind of God.

Rhythm 74

Oh Say, Can You See?
(Inspired by Pastor Vincent Riley)

Oh, say, can you see?
The way our Father planned it to be
To give us a future and give us hope
To depend on Him and not a daily horoscope.
Oh, say, can you see?
What God ordain us to be
The head and not the tail
To conquer and to prevail
Oh, say, can you see?
What is expected of you and of me?
To live life with no regret
To stand tall and pass the test
Oh, say, can you see?
The love the good Father has for you and for me
He sent His Son to save the lost
He sent His Son to die on the cross
Oh, say, can you see?
Jesus rose for you and for me
Defeated the enemy through death, burial, and resurrection
We should be His earthly reflection!

Stage Exit

Let's exit this stage with open eyes and see all that God intended for us to be.

A Change Will Come

I enjoy listening to old school music. One of my favorites is "A Change Will Come" by Otis Redding. One line is: "It's been too hard living but I'm afraid to die I don't know what's up there beyond the sky."

The Bible tells us in 1 John 4:17–18: "As we live in God, our love grows more perfect. So, we will not be afraid on judgement, but we can face Him with confidence because we live like Jesus here in this world. Such *love has no fear* because *perfect love expels all fear.* If we are afraid, it is for fear of punishment, and this shows that we have not *fully experience His perfect love.*"

God gives all of us a "free will." He gives us the chance to choose life (following God's will and His way) or death (following the way of the world). The world paints a picture that shows we should live life the way we want to live it. It tries to convince us that after this life, there's nothing else. That when we die and leave this world that's all there is to it. It paints pretty pictures that show life is a party and that we should party like it's 1999.

As the year 1999 came close to an end, this world was in somewhat of a frenzy. Known as Y2K, some predicted the world would come to an end going into the year 2000 (the millennium). People were told to stock up on food and take all cash out of banks. It was predicted the grid would fail and all computer programming would not operate past December 31, 1999. Fear came into the hearts of billions of people throughout the world. However, we are living proof that those fears were laid to rest, when, as millions participated in Watch Night services, Time Square's drop of the ball and many,

many more New Year's Eve celebrations, as we saw January 1, 2000, come in as a lamb, not the roaring lion the world feared.

God's perfect love cast out all fear, but first, a change must come in our lives. We can't listen to the world's predictions. And we shouldn't let anyone, any circumstances nor any situation, place fear in our lives.

The songwriter said, "It's been too hard living." I will be one of many to say, "Life isn't easy." We face loss of loved ones, sickness and disease, lack and poverty, loneliness and sorrows, just to name a few. In John 10:10 (NLT), Jesus said, "The thief's purpose is to steal, kill and destroy. My purpose is to give them a rich and satisfying life." Thus, we also face joy and happiness, love and peace.

Otis Redding then states, "I'm afraid to die I don't know what's up there beyond the sky."

Philippians 1:21 says, "For to me, to live is Christ, and to die is gain." In this scripture, Paul is stating, if he lives on this earth, he can spread the Gospel of Jesus Christ to more people. But he goes on to say, to die (knowing he has lived for Jesus Christ) is gain because he will be with Jesus.

For those of us who choose to seek the kingdom of God, for those of us who choose to make Jesus Christ our Lord and Savior, there is no need to fear what's beyond the sky; Jesus plainly tells us:

> Let not your heart be troubled; you believe in God, believe also in Me. In my Father's house are many mansions; if it were not so, I would have told you. I go to prepare a place for you (beyond the sky). And if I go and prepare a place for you, I will come again and receive you to Myself; that where I am, there you may be also. (John 14:1-3)

All of us want to live a long, prosperous life. We wish to see our children's children and beyond. Jesus, despite how hard things may be, can make life a beautiful experience, if we allow Him to do so.

Fear has no place in our lives. And if there is fear, allow God's perfect love to enter your life.

A change will come whether we want it or not. It's our choice what the change will be: eternal life or eternal death.

Backdrop 75

Life can throw punches so hard at times until it looks as if God is nowhere to be found. No matter what the crisis is, God is present even in the midst of the storm.

Rhythm 75

He Delayed

God is a God of Mercy; He is a God of Grace
He is a kind loving God; yet He delayed.
How could this be? Doesn't He see me?
I wept and I mourned all night long
The pain was so server; all hope was gone
God is a God of Mercy; He is a God of Grace
He is faithful and He is graceful
He taught us to pray; yet, He chose to delay.
I am Sarah; I prayed, and I prayed
That God will find mercy and give me grace
Yes, I have plenty, but I fill so empty
I am barren, you see; why has God forgotten me?
By this time in life I should be a mother to many
Children in my house, there aren't any
I took it upon myself to gain a son
I learned the hard way; this shouldn't have been done
Thus, I wait; my dream delayed.

I am Joseph; I prayed, and I prayed.
Accused of what I didn't do
My accuser very well knew

That she made a false claim
Didn't even try to clear my name.
I sat in this jail year after year
Some had dreams that brought them fear
I interpreted what one said, "Your freedom is near."
And so, it came, he was set free
My only request, please remember me
I was promised help to set me free
But somehow, he didn't remember me
Now he is gone; I was done wrong
Yet still, I remain strong
So, it came, to this day my very own dream was delayed.

I am an Egyptian; I prayed, and I prayed
That Pharaoh the treachery would release all slaves
For 400 years my people worked in dismay
We prayed to the God of Abraham; yet He delayed

I am Hannah; I prayed, and I prayed
That God would have mercy and give me grace
My heart is torn for no child has been born
To my husband through me can't God see
I prayed; yes, I did; still yet My God delayed

I am David; I prayed, and I prayed
I will admit, mistakes I've made
My baby fell ill; I fast, and I prayed
Yet still, my God delayed

We are Shadrach, Meshach and Abednego
We prayed and we prayed; we refused to go
To the king's table to eat of his feast
Bond in chains our decision the same
As we walked to a furnace turn up high
We prayed, and we prayed not to be thrown inside

But if not for God, we are willing to die
Yes, we prayed but God delayed

I am Jonah, I prayed, and I prayed
Took life in my hand; thus, I disobeyed.
Was swallowed up by a great fish
Three days I remain in this mysterious creature
Because I ran from God's calling of being a preacher
From the very first day I prayed, and I prayed;
Yet still, God delayed

I am Job; I prayed, and I prayed
What did I do to deserve such heartache?
I am blameless and upright in God's sight
I praise His name with all my might
I don't understand this torture I feel
I know I serve a God that's real
This enemy he has put on my track (though he slay me)
Is not playing games; I want my family back
Things look bad; it's made me sad
I prayed and I prayed; my God delayed

I am Daniel; I prayed, and I prayed
For my people in Israel even though they disobeyed
Yet for 21 days no answer in sight
I thought the Lord didn't hear my plight
I waited and I waited for 21 days
I never thought God would delay

I am John; I prayed, and I prayed.
I sit in jail, waiting this day
To be executed for speaking what is right
Against King Herod and his wife
The one that has come, I believe He is the begotten Son.
I waited for Him to save me but the Savior I didn't see.
I prayed, and I prayed but God delayed

I am the woman with the issue of blood
I prayed and I prayed that someone would show me love
Because of my condition it was said to be
Normal people were to stay clear of me
For 12 long years gave all that I had
No more to give but for this reason I live
I knew my healing was on its way
Although it was delayed.

I am Jarius; I prayed, and I prayed
My little girl is sick; this deadly disease has afflicted
Her body with pain; 12 years on this earth will not be in vain
I heard about a man; Jesus is His name
He healed many people; I knew He would do the same
For my dying little girl; she's all I have in this world
I prayed, and I prayed but the healer was delayed.

I am Lazarus; I prayed, and I prayed
I am very sick; my dear sisters ask Jesus to be quick
They feared I would die; they stayed by my side
They prayed and they prayed, but our dear friend was delayed.

Stage Exit

We exit the stage on Isaiah 55:8–9 "For my thoughts are not your thoughts, neither are your ways my ways. As the heavens are higher than the earth, so are my ways higher than your ways and my thoughts than yours." To sum it up, we may see our prayers as being delayed; remember, delayed is not denial.

And even if we don't see it on this side, I believe we will see it on the other side of glory, a place where it can never be taken away from us.

Backdrop 76

God promised to wipe every tear from our eyes. After weeping has endured for the night and joy comes in the morning, we get to a point where enough is enough!

Rhythm 76

Enough Is Enough
(Inspired by Pastor Vincent Riley)

Enough is enough!
I cried my last tear yesterday
Enough is enough!
I give defeat no place to stay
Enough is enough!
I will no longer delay
Enough is enough!
I decided to turn away
Enough is enough!
I choose to obey
Enough is enough!
I will not stray
Enough is enough!
Depression I will lay
Under my feet; it no longer controls me.
Enough is enough; my God rescued me!

Stage Exit

We exit this stage with a sense of boldness and determination. The pity party is over.

The Bible says, "For God so loved the world that He gave His only begotten Son, that whosoever, believes in Him shall not perish but have everlasting life" (John 3:16).

Breaking News, John 3:16 Clarification

It saddens me to know that there are many people in the world that doesn't understand the fullness of this verse. We have religious groups that are constantly debating the one true and living God. Many have different opinions of who Jesus is and as a result, established religious groups to cater to their opinion(s).

There are debates of the skin color of Jesus and where He comes from. I pose this question: If you are drowning or about to burn in a fire or pinned in a car due to a terrible accident, does it matter what the skin color is or the nationality of the person saving you? Jesus saves; that's all that matters.

There are debates of Old Testament versus New Testament. God's Word is the same yesterday, today, and forever.

> For sin shall no longer be your master, because
> you are not under the law, but under grace. What
> then? Shall we sin because we are not under the
> law, but under grace? God forbid. (Romans 6:14)

There are groups that choose to treat the Word of God as if it's like Burger King. The Generation X group and prior should remember the Burger King jingle: "Hold the pickles, hold the lettuce special orders, don't upset us all we ask is that you let us serve it your way." We don't get to have God's Word the way we want it and what fits our opinions.

God created human life as equal; *no one* is better than his neighbor. The scripture says, for God so loved the *world*—the world. So that means all who dwells in the world, God loves. No matter the color of the skin and no matter the country a person comes from, no matter what he/she may have done that was wrong, God still loves us all. He is not pleased with some things we may do, but that doesn't stop Him from loving us. It amazes me how some fail to realize this scripture.

I hope you have your steel toe shoes on because this one may step on a few toes. Here is a translation of John 3:16:

1. God loves the racist as well as the non-racist.
2. In history, God loved the salve masters just as much as he loved the slaves.
3. God loves the foreigner just as much as he loves the domestic.
4. God's love is equal for all race, color, religion, and creed.

If you believe in the Cross, then you must also believe Jesus didn't die for a certain group of people. He was brutally beaten to save *all.* I can't express how important it is for the world to stop having so much hate and hostility for certain groups of people. God loves all and sent His Son as a ransom for all people.

Grace and Mercy

My pastor calls it "The Twin Towers" or "The Wonder Twins." What was he talking about, you might ask? It's grace and mercy. Mercy is God's compassion for us. Mercy is this: "For we have not a high priest which cannot be touched with the feeling of our infirmities; but was tempted as we are, yet without sin" (Hebrews 4:15). In a nutshell, God feels every ache and pain we feel and pours out His mercy upon us.

But this passage is about God's grace: "My Grace is sufficient for you or me" (2 Corinthians 12:9). God's grace is enough for me. While going through a difficult time in my life, I head God say, "My Grace is sufficient for you." When I heard Him speaking to me, I was on the verge of tears; I was angry, frustrated, and disappointed. Then God began to break down His grace as it relates to me. He even gave me a vivid picture.

God said, "What this means is I am covering you. I am your comfort." He assured me it's His love for me and Him hugging me. He showed me Jesus sitting on the throne in His glorious robe. The same robe that has a train so long it fills the temple (Isaiah 6:1). God showed me (through all my tears, anger, frustration, and disappointment) sitting on the lap of Jesus as He sat on the throne. And Jesus took His robe and covered me, cuddled me until I was no longer able to see myself. All I saw was Jesus. He swallowed me up in His robe, and all I felt was peace.

Caught in the Cross Fires

As God gave me the vivid picture of sitting on Jesus's lap, He began to make the situation I was going through clear.

Sometimes, we Christians give way too much credit to the devil. The enemy's assignment is to kill, steal, and destroy. And although this is His assignment, all hardship we go through was not necessarily brought on by the devil. What do I mean by this?

Sometimes, it's our own doing, not the enemy but us, our will and not God's will. Us, having the audacity to try to stand toe-to-toe with God and because we put in us the audacity to stand toe-to-toe with God, we have exalted ourselves high above others.

Sometimes, God gives us an assignment, and because we have our own agenda, we defy and deviate from everything God has instructed us to do. God puts in us a free will. He does not and will not force His will on us; thus, *we* make a choice; it's not always the enemy.

Sometimes, fires start during our defiance. Not because of that old dragons' breath of fire but because of us breathing out fire. Not because the enemy is trying to stop us but because we are stopping ourselves. Why, you ask, would I want to stop myself? The answer: sacrifice! Flesh! And outright disobedience!

Sometimes, we hold on to bad habits because we don't want to endure the transition it will require to let this thing go. We would rather give in to the temptation than fight it.

News flash: the enemy knows your weakness, and when we choose not to fight against our own weaknesses, we have done the job of the enemy. He doesn't have to do anything. He is getting paid for your job well done! Now, understand this: the attack of the enemy comes when you consciously begin to fight the temptation. The enemy recognizes your will to fight back, so that's when he suits up and attacks you. He attacks you when he feels he's about to lose you. When he have you, he doesn't have to fight; all he does is make the pot sweeter, keep baiting you in with all you lust for. *Bam! Pow!*

This is what my good Father showed me:

Sometimes, the defiance fire we breathe catches the innocent in the pathway. This leads to those innocent lives getting burned; some as severe as first degree. So God told me, "This isn't a battle between the person and the enemy. It's a battle between the person and Me, and I am sorrowful that you are caught in the *cross fires,* but My grace will keep you."

Sometimes, we give the enemy too much credit. Give destructive credit where it is due, and from there, change destructive into constructive.

Backdrop 77

The world masquerades sin as being innocent. It advertise it's all in the name of fun or there is no harm in watching this movie or this TV show. There is no harm in listening to this type of music and behaving in this way. Looks can often be deceiving. Some are unaware of the traps set by the enemy. But there are some that go in eyes wide open.

Genesis 39

Now Joseph was well-built and handsome, and after a while, his master's wife took notice of Joseph and said, "Come to bed with me!" But he refused. "With me in charge," he told her, "my master does not concern himself with anything in the house. Everything he owns he has entrusted to my care. No one is greater in this house than I am. My master has withheld nothing from me except you, because you are his wife. How then could I do such a wicked thing and sin against God?" And though she spoke to Joseph day after day, he refused to go to bed with her or even be with her. One day he went into the house to attend to his duties, and none of the household servants was inside. She caught him by his cloak and said, "Come to bed with me!" But he left his cloak in her hand and *ran* out of the house.

Rhythm 77

Run, Run
(Inspired by Bishop T.D. Jakes)

Run, run as fast as you can
To kill, steal, and destroy is the enemy's plan
You can't control this; it's sin, my friend
Listen to godly counsel; it's not hard to comprehend
You are fooling yourself when you choose not to see
The grips of sin therefore, I beseech
Fall to your knees; prayer is the key
Repent of all ungodliness; you will be set free
Temptation will knock at every door;
It's the enemy my friend, coming to settle the score
Sin tries to control you; put you at its command
It entices you and fights you until you give in
Its ultimate goal is bringing your life to an end
Run, run as fast as you can, least it catches you
Destroying your destiny, my friend.

Stage Exit

Before exiting this stage, let's take a close look at ourselves and the choices we make. If our life choices aren't glorying God, then we should make a conscious decision to do an about face, repent of our sin, turn from our wicked ways, take up our cross, and follow Jesus.

Backdrop 78

And since you know that he cares, let your language show
it. Don't add words like "I swear to God" to your own word.
Don't show your concocting impatience by concocting
oaths to hurry up God. Just say yes or no. Just say what is
true. That way, your language can't be used against you.

—James 5:12 (MSG)

My pastor, Vincent Riley, says, "Your video ought to match your
audio." Pastor Joel Osteen says, "Children are like little video cam-
eras walking around." There is a saying, "Say what your mean and
mean what you say."

I am one of many managers of a call center. Two important
guidelines we teach our customer service representatives are: set
expectations and don't give false hope. Basically, this means, advise
the customer upfront what the company can or cannot do with
assisting in their concerns. And for the most part, what the customer
wants is not what they qualify for or what the company is able to
accommodate. Of course, this makes the customer upset or angry,
but if we state the company's final position, there is no issue.

The next thing is don't give false hope. What this means is don't
tell the customer they will get what they want to avoid them from
becoming irate or to avoid an uncomfortable conversation. We teach
to stand the company's ground even if it's not what the customer
wants to hear. So many times, in our daily lives, we make promises
not kept. Some of us honestly try to keep our word. For instance,

we made a promise to pay a bill and had full intentions of fulfilling that promise, but something happened, and our money starts looking funny.

But there are times when we make promises we have no intention of keeping. The following poem is to make us think, "Am I doing my best to speak truth, or am I only saying what the other person wants to hear? Am I walking the walk and talking the talk?" In other words, "Am I a man or woman of my word?"

Rhythm 78

Between

Between what you say and what you do; does the image of God look good on you?

Between what you say and what you do; does the word of truth reside in you?

Between what you say and what you do; can your family and friends depend on you?

Between what you say and what you do; are you leaving a straight path for others to follow you?

Between what you say and what you do; can your children say "I want to be like you?"

Between what you say and what you do; if you evaluated yourself, does your conscience guide you?

Stage Exit

Upon exiting this stage, did this performance make you think between what you say and what you do?

The Good Son

In 1993, Macaulay Culkin starred in a movie called *The Good Son*. Culkin played a character named Henry. His cousin Mark comes to live with Henry and his family after the death of his mother, but Mark's stay turns out to be one of disbelief. Mark witnesses Henry do things that were extremely disturbing. Henry kills a neighbor's dog, he caused two accidents, one that nearly kills his sister while ice skating. And another that nearly caused motorists to die after he drops what appears to be a human body off an overpass bridge.

At the end of the movie, Henry tires to kill his mom first then Mark as they scuffle near the edge of a cliff. Henry's mom sees the scuffle, and just as she makes her way to the boys, they both fall over, but she catches them. Holding on to each boy, one holding on to one hand and the other boy the other hand. Even while hanging over the ledge, Henry tries to convenience his mom he needs both her hands, that she should let go of his cousin and let him fall to his death.

The struggle is getting harder to hold both boys, and she must make a choice as to which boy to let go of so she could pull the other to safety. Her tough decision resulted in letting go of her own son and pulling her nephew to safety.

The end of this movie reminds me of how many people try to hold on to the world with one hand and God with the other. And just as the mother in this movie struggles to decide which to let go of, so it is with people today.

This is a dangerous place to allow one's self to be. What many people refuse to realize is this: you must let one go. You must decide as to which brings life and which takes life. In the movie, no matter how cute Henry was, no matter how innocent he looked and no matter how sweet he sounded, his intensions were always evil.

No matter how cute the world makes it look, no matter how innocent it seems and no matter how sweet the offer sounds, if it's not in God's hand, it's in the world's hand, and you want to let those things go.

You must visualize yourself hanging off a cliff. You look up and see God with His hand extended out to help, but you also see the hand of the enemy. Who are you going to trust? So before your life is hanging in the balance, make the choice to hold on to God's unchanging hand and allow Him to pull you to safety.

Backdrop 79

The Bible tells us in Genesis 1:1, "In the beginning God created the heavens and the earth." And John 1:1 says, "In the beginning was the word and the word was with God and the word was God."

Rhythms 79

God Exists
(Inspired by Bishop T.D. Jakes)

How do I describe what I cannot see?
How do I embrace what's not visible to me?
How do I listen when there is no sound?
How can I be free when it looks like I am bound?
How can I feel what I cannot touch?
How can I believe when I don't have much?
The way I describe what I cannot see is to show the love the Savior give to me.
The way I embrace what's not visible to me is worship the God of how all things came to be.
The way I listen when there is no sound is spending time meditating when no one else is around.
The way to feel free when it looks like I am bound is to remember the thorns Jesus wore as a crown.
The way I feel what I cannot touch is through the spirit; God loves us so much.
The way I believe when I don't have much is remember, Jesus paid it all; He was obedient to God's call.

Stage Exit

Always remember and don't ever forget, God exists before anything created on the earth. Look around; you see Him moving through the trees, and you see Him through all the wonders of this world.

Backdrop 80

Many years ago, I completed a Bible study course created by Dr. Tony Evans called, "The Horizonal Jesus." One point discussed in the lesson was the difference between a function and a source. An example given by Dr. Tony Evans was a water faucet. The faucet is the function, but the water is the source. So the faucet is the function that delivers the source. It's disheartening when some of us put more emphasis on the function and little to no emphasis on the source.

Rhythm 80

But God
(Inspired by Dr. Tony Evans)

Cells and muscles, sinew and skin is a function of how life begins;
    but God is the source.
The blood that runs warm through our veins is a function for life;
    but God is the source.
The heart that beats in rhythm in our chest is a function for life; but
    God is the source.
The air we breathe is a function of life; but God is the source.
The water we drink is a function of life; but God is the source.
The food we eat is a function of life; but God is the source.

Stage Exit

We exit this stage leaving carnality behind; nothing is possible
unless the Lord says so.

Backdrop 81

Jesus never told us that following Him would be easy. In fact, when we make the decision to follow Jesus, I believe, is when the greatest attacks come in our lives. But God! While sitting on my front porch meditating on the goodness of God one day, He showed me how things the enemy set up to kill us at times was the very thing that saves us.

Rhythm 81

The Killing Function

81-1 It Was Meant to Kill

My life gets hard at times
It was then the enemy tried to confine
The deepest part and the surface of my mind
But oh, the good Father is so kind!
He commands grace and mercy to follow me;
Although my eyes couldn't see.
The enemy threw everything at me he could;
He thought that I would
Lay down and allow him to have me bound;
By his threats and my regrets;
That once so easily beset me in so much mess;
I must admit he made me sweat.
But I finally came to the cross;
Jesus saves the lost; and what was so amazing too
Is that it came to be; the function design to kill
Was actually God's will and became the source
That saved my life, the reason why I survived.

81-2 The River

So, for three months they hid me
Because male babies were thrown in the Nile river
God had not yet sent a deliver
As time came to pass, hiding me could no longer last
My mother made a basket for me;
Hide me in the river amongst the reeds
Pharaoh's daughter found me
Then had her maid remove me
And so, it came to be
The river that was meant to kill me
Was the same river that saved me.

81-3 The Cross

What is it that I have done?
Me, being the begotten son
So many people scandalized my name
Seeking ways to bring me shame
Don't they realize this can't be done?
I am the only begotten Son
False accusations, constant attacks
Bounty hunters are on my track
Sadducees, Pharisees, Chief and High Priest
Trying their best to bring me grief.
If only they knew the Gospel truth
This constant disbelief they must cease.
They schemed, they plotted, but deep down they knew
All I was accused of wasn't true.
I was condemned to be nailed to a rugged cross
At which time they thought my life would be lost
But the very thing the thought would kill me
Was the very thing God used to set the saved free
In their eyes the cross was a killing source
But what they did reinforced

What was foretold by prophets of old
That rugged cross saves souls.

Stage Exit

Let's exit the stage with this thought in mind: some trials come to make us stronger.

It Was...

(Inspired by Bishop T.D. Jakes)

It was designed to make you think.

It was designed to make you pray.

It was designed to make you look inside yourself.

It was designed to make you draw closer to God.

During his ministry, Jesus taught a lot through parables.

And for the most part, not only did the multitude not understand what he was saying; neither did his disciples.

The words of God etched in the Bible were not necessarily created to leap off the pages with clear understanding.

Some scriptures are but some aren't.

Some scriptures were designed to make you wonder.

Some were designed to make you say, "God, I don't understand."

Some were designed to make you thirsty and hungry for God.

Some were designed to make you simply stop and make time for God.

Can we take what is new and join it to what is old?

No, God makes all things new.

Do we take a lamp and place it under the stand, or do we place it on top of the stand so that it does what it was designed to do and shine light to overpower the darkness?

Do we build our homes on the first piece of ground we see? Or do we make certain it's built on a solid foundation?

When we find what is good and worthy, valuable and priceless, life changing and everlasting, do we ignore it? Or do we give up all we have to obtain it?

Jesus spoke through many parables to help bring to light all that is in darkness.

Backdrop 82

The Bible gives accounts of wrong that was done to good people—not perfect people, but good people. The ones that were wronged had the opportunity to get revenge on those that did wrong, but instead, they did as Jesus said and "turned the other cheek" (Matthew 5:38).

Rhythm 82

I'm Not Like That
(Inspired by Bishop T.D. Jakes)

Genesis 25–27
82-1

You planned, and you schemed at my weak point of the day.
Made a savory stew sending temptation my way.
And yes, I could've resisted, but my mind didn't think that way.
At my point of lust, I gave my birth right away.
You took what belong to me; it made me angry I must say;
I packed up my belongings and went about my way.
Despite what was done, I am the firstborn son; God blessed my home to prosper,
He saw me second to none.
I sent you a message; I heard fear came to your heart;
You thought I was out to get you; revenge is not in my heart.
The thing that was done, I will say it was wrong.
I'm not trying to get you back because *I'm not like that.*

Genesis 37
82-2

I wore a coat of many colors;
Because of that you and the others
Took my life and sold it away;
Told our daddy I died that day.
You see me as you think I should be;
The basis of your conclusion is how you treated me.
But *I'm not like that;* I wouldn't do what you did;
What you meant for harm, God forbid.

1 Samuel 19
82-3

You chased me, and you stalked me trying to take my life away.
I don't understand it; I've honored you to this day.
You entered the cave to give yourself relief;
What you didn't realize I could've brought you much grief.
For in the background was where I stood
Watching everything you did; most would say, I should;
Use the opportunity; bring your life to an end
Oh, but I knew that would be sin
And although I could've gotten you back
I'm here to say, *I'm not like that*

Stage Exit

We are supposed to treat others the way we want to be treated.
The saints of old said, "Two wrongs don't make a right." Let's exit
this stage taking a lesson from Esau, Joseph, and David. God will
make right all that was done wrong to us.

350

Where did you lay your Lazarus?

> Then, when Mary came where Jesus was, and saw Him, she fell at His feet, saying to Him, "Lord, if You had been here, my brother would not have died." Therefore, when Jesus saw her weeping and the Jews who came with her weeping, He groaned in the spirit and was troubled. And He said, "Where have you laid him?" (John 11:32–33)

When I read the story of Lazarus, I wondered why Jesus asked the question, "Where have you laid him?" I prayed and asked God to help me understand why Jesus asked this question. Doesn't He know all? Through spending time with God, meditating on His word, He answered my prayer.

Reading the Bible takes time and dedication. I think the Word of God was given to man in a way that it creates a hunger that pushes us to dig a little deeper to get a full understanding of its content. There were many times in the Bible where Jesus gave a parable or made a statement, and His disciples didn't understand what was said. Jesus would then explain in a way the disciples would understand. Read John 11:1–14 (NKJV). I will meet you here once you are done.

Good to see you back so soon. After reading this scripture, in modern-day time, if you would allow me to use my imagination, Jesus would've said, "Duh, do you not comprehend anything I say? Were you not with me when I said, 'The girl is not dead but asleep?'

(Matthew 9:24 concerning Jarius's daughter) Did I not raise her? The same has happened with Lazarus." I can see Jesus now, walking away and shaking His head saying, "Help 'em, Father."

Let's look at the accounts leading up to Lazarus's death. Word from Martha and Mary was sent to Jesus concerning their brother Lazarus's illness. The sisters expected Jesus to come right away because of the close relationship they shared (John 11:3–7). Notice, the scripture states, "He whom You love is sick." Why did the sisters make it a point to say he whom you love? Doesn't Jesus love everyone? Well, I believe it was because of the closeness of the relationship.

The house of Mary and Martha was not like the houses in Holes and Nest; this was a house Jesus was welcomed. This was a house where, if Jesus needed a place to lay His head, this was it. This was a house where Jesus had a good home-cooked meal.

God revealed to me that raising Lazarus from the dead played a vital part in the cross. Why? Because of John 11:53: "Then, from that day on, they plotted to put Him to death."

Once reaching the place where Mary and Martha were, Jesus asked "Where did you lay him?" (John 11:33). Mary and Martha immediately though of a physical laying down. And, reading the scripture, I thought the same. However, God gave understanding to me. James 1:5: "If any of you lack wisdom, let him ask of God.

Jesus was asking, "At what point did you stop believing I am all powerful? At what point did you give up? At what point did you lose faith?" Find the answer to these questions and that is where you laid your Lazarus.

Backdrop 83

Our God is a mighty God. He is the Alpha and Omega, the beginning and the end. He is a loving and kind God, and He loves us so much He came in the flesh (Jesus) to save us. He deserves all glory and all honor. We should praise and worship His holy name always.

Rhythm 83

"Say My Name"

I Am not the Big Guy in the sky.
You insult Me with this lie.
I Am not the man upstairs.
I Am the one whom you can cast all your cares.
I Am not a simple moment of silence.
I Am your everything; your alliance.
I Am not your last resort; all plans before Me you must abort.
I Am not to be used for swearing; instead you should be sharing,
My Gospel, the good news.
This is what you can use to draw nations close to Me.
For on the last day all will fall to their knees and confess that Jesus is
Lord, the final say once and for all.

Stage Exit

My prayer is that we leave this stage with more reverence for a
mighty and holy God.

Backdrop 84

The Bible gives many names for God, but it is not to be mistaken to say there is more than one God. There is only one true living God.

Rhythm 84

Me and My Shadow; El Shaddai

Yea though I walk through the valley of the shadow
of death, I shall fear no evil: for thou art with me;
thy rod and thy staff they comfort me.

—Psalm 23

Me and My Shadow sit on the porch; we watch as He cause the wind
to rustle through the trees; sitting there enjoying each other's
company and the coolness of His breeze.

Me and My Shadow sit close to the shoreline. Watching the waves as
they roll in, feeling the coolness of the ocean's breeze.

Me and My Shadow sit and admire the mountaintop. Taking in the
looks of the sun peaking over all My Shadow has done.

Me and My Shadow have walked during the cool of the morning. He
listens as I tell Him my story.

Me and My Shadow have midnight talks; He calms my soul as I
watch the clock.

My Shadow is my everything:

He is Jehovah Jireh; my provider

He reminds me the enemy is a liar

He is Jehovah Shalom; my peace

He is the one that give me sleep
He is Jehovah Rapha; my healer
He holds the keys to lock up the one who steals.

Stage Exit

We exit this stage with the Shadow of El Shaddai over us.

Backdrop 85

We must realize that there is a real devil after us. He is not like the image shown on the bottles of Texas Pete, in a red suit and a pitchfork in his hand. He is angry, and he is out for vengeance. He will trick all that isn't rooted and grounded in Jesus Christ. The Bible tells us in 2 Corinthians 10:4–6 (NKJV), "For the weapons of our warfare *are* not carnal but mighty in God for pulling down strongholds, casting down arguments and every high thing that exalts itself against the knowledge of God, bringing every thought into captivity to the obedience of Christ, and being ready to punish all disobedience when your obedience is fulfilled."

Rhythm 85

Weapons

The enemy knows what weapons to use; he watches you, he studies
   you, then makes his move.
He presents to you what he knows you want; he dresses it up and
   then it flaunts.
He knows what it takes to bring you down; he throws a blow that
   knocks you to the ground.
And just as you were about to get up, he whispers to you, "Give up.
"You can't handle this, I'm more powerful than you."
He very well knows the things you do.
He watches your life; he knows this too, that you have pushed God
   away from you.
So, there you are standing in full view; you haven't asked the Father
   to cover you.
There you are, he sees what you do; you dabble in the world, so he
   makes it easy for you.
To get all the things you lust for and desire; he knows you enjoy
   playing with fire.
The enemy knows what weapons to use; he keeps them in stock and
   then he pursues; he catches you off guard and reels you in; thus,
   begins a life of sin.

The enemy knows who to choose; he knows your life he knows you
didn't choose.

Stage Exit

Before we exit this stage, know who the enemy is and know
there is no way to win without God going before you.

Backdrop 86

Exodus 1 tells the story of how the children of Israel were mighty in the land of Egypt; yet they were slaves of the Egyptians. This is what the Bible says concerning God's people: "The weak shall say, I am strong; the poor shall say, I am rich. We are the head and not the tail; we are above and not beneath; we are more than conquers through Christ Jesus."

Rhythm 86

The Majority Rules

If we would only stick together, oh, what great and mighty things we would do! We are the majority; this I know is true. How do we allow the lesser one to lead us into captivity? It's not always about strength or how strong we think we may be. But it's all about our mind-set; that's the key for being free.

The children of Israel back down. They allow the Egyptians to beat them down. It's sad but it is true; they didn't realize they were the majority as they grew, mighty before the Egyptians in the land. But the Egyptian king knew the truth. Out of fear he declared, "We should make life hard for them to bear. Deal harshly with them, make them scared. All of them will be our slaves. It's obvious to me that they don't see their strength in numbers could overpower me."

Stage Exit

So when God's people are ignorant to the truth, the snares of the enemy will overpower you. The late Bishop G.E. Patterson said, "The truth can only set you free if you know it and then apply it."

Backdrop 87

We have a misconception of why Jesus came to earth. Matthew 10:34 records this: "Do not suppose that I have come to bring peace to the earth. I did not come to bring peace, but a sword. For I have come to turn a man against his father, a daughter against her mother, a daughter-in-law against her mother-in-law."

This means Jesus represents truth, righteousness, and all that is holy. But not everyone stands for what Jesus stands for, thus causing division and conflict. And although Jesus is holy, there were many ungodly things going on that made Him angry. Anger is a natural emotion. The Bible in Ephesians 4:26 says to be angry but do not allow angry to cause sin. Jesus felt the emotion of anger, yet He didn't sin; He came to set things straight.

Rhythm 87

Jesus Came

87-1

Jesus came to tear up some things
Entered the temple one day
He was truly dismayed
As He stood and checked out the scene
He wasn't happy with what was seen
In the temple; the house of God
Merchants were selling; with no regards
To what was sacred and what was holy
Read your Bible; it tells the story
Of how Jesus turned tables over.
Doves were being sold; money was exchanged
Jesus stopped this unlawful gain
He made it clear to all who would hear
That where they stood was a house of prayer.

87-2

Jesus came to stir up some things
Sadducees and Pharisees always complained

Debating about this and questioning that
Always trying to put Jesus to the test
They argued and bickered about the Law
Truth of the matter; they stood in awe
Of all the things Jesus did
Many people couldn't comprehend
All the signs and wonders done
If only they had realized he is the begotten Son.

Stage Exit

I guess it can be said Jesus was somewhat of a radical. He stood on the word of God, no matter what!

Backdrop 88

The book of Joshua tells us that after all the signs and wonders God did leading the Israelites out of captivity, there came a generation that knew absolutely nothing about him. Reason being is no one who knew took the time to tell them.

Rhythm 88

Show Me the Way

How can it be; I just don't understand
How an entire generation forgot the mighty hand
Of God, our Father and all that was done
Lead the Israelites out of slavery
Through the leadership of Moses's bravery
First were the plagues; ten of them came
God spoke His word; all of Egypt was disturbed
Towards the last sign and wonder
Pharaoh's blunder caused him to turn away
From all God sent Moses to say
But when the firstborn was killed
Pharaoh realized the God of the Israelites is real
He commanded they leave, as he bereaved
the loss of his firstborn son and all God had done.
They made it to the Red Sea
Then things got rough;
Coming up behind them was Pharaoh; he was tough
Facing a raging sea; no one could perceive
How they would get cross; they thought all hope was lost

But God had a plan, said to Moses, "Use the rod in your hand?
Stretch it across the sea, then you and the Israelites shall see,
that I am the Lord your God; it's me or nothing at all."
Through the power of God's mighty hand, Moses lifted his hand,
and they walked on dry land, thus I don't understand, how it
came to be an entire generation chose not to seek the power and
love of God and the miracle of Moses's rod.
So, we come to the present day; who is willing to show the way?
We have a generation that doesn't know God. A generation that
choose not to follow His call. Do they realize this leads to a
downfall?
Refusing to die to self; how many are left?
That's willing to say, "Hey, that's not the way. Walk with me, talk
with me, let's pray together to our God in heaven.

Stage Exit

We exit this stage with grieved hearts, thinking about how so
many people have turned their backs on God. Be willing to show
people the greatness of a great and merciful God.

Backdrop 89

God has a plan for our lives. He is a good Father and knows what is best for us. Just as in the natural, every good parent will do what is best for their child(ren). There are times we think our way is faster and better. Some even believe they are helping God. 2 Samuel 6:6 (NLT) tells the story of Uzzah trying to help God. "When they came to the threshing floor of Nacon, Uzzah reached out and took hold of the ark of God, because the oxen stumbled. The LORD's anger burned against Uzzah because of his irreverent act; therefore, God struck him down, and he died there beside the ark of God." It is my opinion that Uzzah thought he was doing a good thing, but it turned out to not work in his favor. Even during troubled times, we should let God be God.

Rhythm 89

The Hard Way

I learned the hard way, that if I am to make it through any day, my only choice is to listen to what God say.

I have learned this day, to keep my hands off God's plan. Because He knows what's best for me, those things my blinded eyes can't see. A hedge of protection He made for me, if I choose to sit at His feet. And listen to His word, because at times, life left me perturbed.

I have learned the hard way to listen and obey, to all the good Father has to say. Had I done this from the beginning, I would not have allowed the enemy to lead me into the wilderness, where my flesh is drawn to bitterness.

You know, things didn't go as I planned, so that's why I put my hands, on what only God can do. Don't look like that; you've done it too.

Wondering aimlessly for years, oh yes, I've shed many tears. Even screamed and stomped a time or few; don't look so altogether, you probably did it too.

I have learned to never forget, that a life of regrets, is not what God has planned for me. I am His own. He comforts me.

I put my grubby hands on God's perfect plan, thus delaying my victory, my excuse, my blinded eyes couldn't see. So I walked around lost, oh my goodness, I paid a hefty cost. The sad thing you see, Jesus had already paid it for me.

Time wasted, heart breaking, for oh so many years, and I didn't want to admit but with it came fear.

I'm learning to take my hands off God's plan. He is the beginning and the end; He made a way for me to live without sin. It was hard to see; God didn't need me, trying to make His plan move faster; it seems I forgot He is the Master of things above and below. Believe me, I know, that this thing is not about me but about having faith in what my blinded eyes cannot see.

Stage Exit

Let's leave this stage making a commitment to let go and let God do what only God can do. Remember rhythm number one: "From God to Us." Everything we need is found in God, our good Father.

Backdrop 90

The last chapter of the gospels are bittersweet to me. The eleven disciples who spent the past three years of their lives with Jesus, they listened to Him, saw Him crucified and died on a cross. Although Jesus foretold He would be raised on the third day, I imagine moments after Jesus's removal off the cross was heartbreaking. I imagine the next day, reality set in: "Jesus isn't here." This had to be a bitter moment. Then while on a boat fishing, Jesus called to the disciples from the shore. Once they realized it was Jesus and made it back to shore, they had a fish fry and ate breakfast with Jesus, all while looking at the beauty of God's great creation: the ocean and the sunrise—sweet! They spent time with Jesus again, but they watched as He ascended into the heavens. Now, to watch Jesus die, be separated from Him for a couple of days and then watch Him leave again and be separated from seeing Him face-to-face again; this would've been the ultimate bittersweet moment for me.

Rhythm 90

A Leader
(Inspired by Bishop T.D. Jakes)

Peter, you are a leader; all the disciples are following you.
But this I must say, catching fish is not what I told you to do.
You first saw me at the Sea of Galilee;
I said, "Come, follow me."
You were a fisherman by trade
I made you a fisher of men.
You were the first to proclaim me as Messiah,
Son of the living God.
You were the only one who walked on the water once you heard me
  call.
You were the first to promise never to turn away;
It was you who recognized through Me is the only way.
You were the one who thought that you were defending me.
Cut off the ear of the one that came to arrest me
You were the only one to jump off the boat
Swimming your way to me;
All the others rowed back from the sea.
Yes, you made mistakes, but that didn't take away
From what I called you to be; come off the sea
And take possession of who you were ordained to be;

A fisher of men; you can live without sin.
Peter, you are a leader; do you love me?
You answered, "Yes, Lord."
I say, "Then feed my sheep."

Stage Exit

Close your eyes and imagine the sounds of the waves across the sea and the smell of fresh salt water. A cool breeze comes from the sea spreading the delicious smells of fresh water fish frying. You and the others talk to Jesus waiting to eat breakfast as the sun rises because the ultimate Son rose as promised.

Backdrop 91

I enjoy the game of football. I am a Carolina Panthers' fan, somewhat new to the game. If I had to describe my level of knowledge, I would say I'm in middle school. I like to win and don't take losing well; I think it's called a "sore loser." I'm not claiming this, but I think that's what it's called. Any who, I enjoy making it to the playoffs; even more so, I enjoy having home advantage. With home advantage, you are operating in your realm, on your turf, in what is familiar and most of all, surrounded by thousands of supportive fans opposed to a few when playing on the opponent's turf. You are a part of the majority. While thinking of this, God showed me that too many of us are fighting the enemy, not realizing we have home advantage.

Rhythm 91

Home Advantage

We wrestle not against flesh and blood;
The enemy comes in like a flood.
He use his wiles trying to bait us in
He lives in darkness, consumed with sin
He disguises himself as a beam of light
Try to mesmerize us so we lose our sight.
His home turf is darkness indeed
He pushes and he pressures with hopes we concede;
He has a plan; thus, he proceeds.
To drag us in and sift us like wheat
His focused goal: lead us to defeat.
Listen, my friend, this I say:
Don't allow the enemy to deceive you this way.
Gird up your loins, have your breastplate intact
Please recognize it's a vicious attack.
We are in a battle; it is the Lord's.
Stay in his word; don't be disturbed.
We won't let that old dragon pull us in
We will stand in God's light; the fight begins.
We march out to the battlefield
God goes before us; the enemy revealed

We stand in unison, fighting on our turf
Proclaiming what's ours, dominion of the earth.

Stage Exit

We exit this stage, but it's not the end. We will not allow the enemy to have any advantage over our lives while we live in this earthly realm.

Backdrop 92

How many of us have been in relationships and heard or said, "It's not you, it's me"? This is usually done because we recognize our faults, and this statement may be a way of apologizing. On the other hand, it's sometimes an easy escape. In the following poem, it's a way of recognizing the mistakes made with my relationship with a faithful Jesus.

Rhythm 92

It's Not You, It's Me

We've been in this relationship since the beginning of time
Yet I search and search trying to find.
What I'm searching for I should already know; you gave to me, but I
    keep searching for more.
Here I am on my knees recognizing, it's not you, it's me.
There's no one else that can love me like you do;
Yet still I continue to pursue things of this world that only hurt me.
Here I am, hear my plea, it's not you, it's me.
I don't want to lose this peace I've found.
But circumstances and situations keep me bound.
I know You will never leave, nor forsake me
But still I keep searching for more, it's not you it's me.
I have no right asking you believe; it's not you, it's me.
I ask that you forgive me when I go astray,
Doing things that caused me to disobey.
Forgiveness by nature is what you do, but there are things I must do,
    too.
Put all my trust and rely on You; this I know is true
It's not me, it's all about you.

Stage Exit

God is the exact place He was when we first came to Him. He didn't move; we did.

Backdrop 93

I take everyday living and find significance in it. I listen for simple spoken words to help me be a better person. To wash, means to make clean, and to condition means to soften. Our hearts must be cleansed of all that is not like God. And for all the unforgiveness, disappointments, anger, and bitterness, for all the disbelief and rebellion we have allowed to come in can cause us to harden our hearts. We need to allow God to condition all those things and make it soft again.

Rhythms 93

My Heart

Wash and condition my heart
I need to make a clean start
Taking off the mask
And let go of things from the past
Scrape away the residue
It hinders me from praising You
I'm tired of this thing I do
Falling prey to the enemy
He brings nothing new
It seems I should learn
Your word says cast all my concern
On You because You care for me
But a breakthrough I cannot see
Wash and condition my heart
I need to make a fresh start
From the heart flows the issues of life
At times I live mine in strife
My desire is to be free
Of all that controls me
Disappointments hit hard
And catch me off guard

Sometimes I get overwhelmed
I'm then compelled to take matters in my hands
Instead of taking a stand against flesh and my way
I surrender my life to You, Lord, for the rest of my days.

Stage Exit

The heart is the center of our being. It's the source that pumps life throughout our bodies.

From My Heart to Yours

In conclusion, our very lives depend on surrendering to God's will. Outside of God, we can do nothing. His Word is true and everlasting. Our feelings about His Word doesn't change the fact, as Jesus said, "it is written." God gives us a free will. He gave us a brain to decide right from wrong. And guess what? He's not going to make us choose right from wrong. He placed before us choices: life or death, blessings or curses, and gives us the answer.

God plainly tells us which to choose but will not make us choose. FYI, to not make a decision is a decision. We must make a bold stand and not be ashamed of the Gospel of Jesus. Is it possible to be in two places at once? Is it possible to go to the left and to the right at the same time? No, we must make a choice.

God has great plans for us—plans to have a hope and a future, to prosper and to have an abundant life. He promised to never leave us nor forsake us. He promised to be with us, even until the end of time, and time will never end.

All the above come with conditions. In 2 Chronicles 7:14, the Word of God says, "If my people (Christians), which are called by my name [*to go to all the nations and preach the gospel to the world so that all will be His people*], shall humble themselves [*realize that without God, we are nothing*] and pray and seek my face [*do not forsake the assembly of ourselves together; do not be anxious about anything, but in everything by prayer and supplications with thanksgiving let your request be made know to God, seek him while he can be found*] and turn from their wicked ways, [*selfish pride, prejudice, un-forgiveness, hatred, self-righteousness, and my way attitudes. We must die to self*] then will

I hear from heaven, [*Jesus is forever interceding, but only if we come to Him. And angels are sent on undercover assignments; how are we treating people. What are angles saying about us in heaven*] and will forgive their sin; [*notice it's singular, not sins plural because everything we do that goes against God is sin; rather it's one thing or many. And there is no big sin or little sin; it's all sin, the wages of sin is death*].

And heal the land [*senseless killings, all kinds of abuse, sickness and disease, depression* and oppression will end]."

The choice is simple: *choose life*. Remember, we will spend eternity somewhere; it's up to us where.

About the Author

Mona Goodman Harry was raised in a small community known as St. John located in Lynchburg, South Carolina. She developed a joy for writing at the age of thirteen years old. Mona is described as having "an old soul" because of her old-fashioned ways and her love for classic television shows and movies. Her Christian upbringing began at home with her parents and grandparents. Mona attended Asbury United Methodist Church located in Lynchburg, South Carolina, until she relocated to Charlotte, North Carolina. During her childhood, not one summer went by without a couple of weeks of vacation Bible school.

In 1995, Mona dedicated her life to Jesus Christ. In 1999, God put in her heart the desire to write poetry that would teach people of His undying love, grace, and mercy. God gave to her the title *Rhythms for the Soul*. Mona learned a valuable lesson early in life, and that was to guard people's heart and show compassion. She believes that Christians should never cease interceding for each other. Mona believes people (especially Christians) should be vigilant (recognizing when things aren't quite right), transparent (ready to give a testimony), and always on guard to encourage others.

Mona is the wife of Pomanda Harry and mother of Amanda Monique and William Thomas Harry. Outside of writing poetry, Mona enjoys worshipping at Meeting Place Church (MPC) where she is under the leadership of Pastor Vincent H. Riley and First Lady, Lydia Riley. She also enjoys singing with the United Voices of Praise at MPC.

CPSIA information can be obtained
at www.ICGtesting.com
Printed in the USA
FSHW010646200521
81561FS